皆様、

はじめまして！　Eric Hawkinson　（エッリク・ハーキンソン）と申します。　２０１１年に福知山に引っ越しました。これで三回目の来日となります。最初に日本に来た時は関西外国語大学に一年間留学をしました。その時は関西の文化を少し習いました。でももっと多くを教わりたいです。二回目は京都府の宮津市教育委員会で５年間ぐらい働きました。今年も本当に興奮しています。　福知山はとてもきれいな町だと思います。私は米国のアリゾナ州からきました。アリゾナで有名な物はグランド・キャニオン、サボテン、本当に暑い夏です。　兄弟は二人だけです。弟と父はアリゾナに住んでいます。趣味は天文学、コンピュータ、映画、音楽、お酒、スポーツですが、新しい日本の趣味を探しています。道で歩いている時やレストランで食べている時に私を見かけたら何か話しかけてください。　皆様とお会いすることを楽しみしています。　今年の私の目標は成美大学生に英語についてわくわくさせたり、米国と日本の関係をより良くしたり、したいと思います。　そして次が一番重要なポイントですが、楽しんでたくさん新しい友達に会いたいです。それで…Let's be friends!　一緒に阪神タイガスのゲームを見たり、すもうを見に行ったり、公園に行ったりしましょう！

私はあなたに現在の雇用市場で成功するために必要なすべてのコミュニケーションツールを学んで欲しいです。あなたが
　　<u>英語を使わなければ、どんどん忘れてしまいます。</u>
日常生活に英語を取り入れてみることで最終的に<u>英語と一つとなっていきます</u>。

I want to make sure you have all the communication tools you will need to succeed in tomorrow's job market. My biggest suggestion is to try to incorporate English into your daily life because…

　　　　<u>If you don't use it, you lose it.</u>

When you use it every day, you eventually become
<u>One with English</u>.

erichawkinson.com
erichawkinson@gmail.com
YouTube: ericcharleshawkinson
Twitter: @eric_hawkinson
facebook.com/tidehawk

Visit the website and download the app!

コースのホームページまたアプリケーションで復讐しましょう！

togetherlearning.com

Table of Contents
One with English

#	Topic		Page
0	My Fundamentals	基盤を作ろう	1
1	My Self-Introduction	私の自己紹介	11
2	My First Chat	私の最初のチャット	25
3	My Room	私の部屋	39
4	My New Friends	友達を作ろう	55
5	My Family	私の家族	65
6	My Schedule	私のスケジュール	73
7	My Day Off	私の休日	81
8	My Neighbourhood	私の近所	89
9	My Driver's Test	私の運転免許試験	97
10	My Hobbies	私の趣味	105
11	My Favourite Thing	私の好きなもの	113
12	My House Growing Up	私の育った家	121
13	My Nightmare	私の悪夢	129

STAGE ZERO

My foundation
基盤を作ろう

テーマ：	Theme:
なぜ英語が必要ですか？	Why is English important?
コース紹介	Course Introduction
コースの準備	Course Preparation

Hi, I'm Eric. Nice to meet you.
How are you? I'm OK, and you?

文法：	Grammar:
授業の表現	Classroom Expressions

Can you repeat that please?
I don't understand.

ローマ字	Romaji

Matsui Hideki
komputa

アルファベット	Alphabet

A B C D *E* F G H *I* J K L M N *O* P Q R S T *U* V W X Y Z

母音と子音の発音	vowel and consonant sounds

/a/ /e/ /i/ /o/ /u/

Stage 0 — One with English コミュニケーションコ

My foundation 基盤を作ろう

Why is English important? 何で英語が必要ですか？

- English is the most widespread language in the world and is more widely spoken and written than any other language.　英語は世界の一番使っている言語です。
- Over 400 million people use the English vocabulary as a mother tongue, only surpassed in numbers, but not in distribution by speakers of the many varieties of Chinese.　４０億人は英語が母語です。世界の２番目です。
- Over 700 million people, speak English, as a foreign language.　世界で７０億人が英語が話せます。
- Did you know that of all the world's languages (over 2,700) English is arguably the richest in vocabulary; and that the Oxford English Dictionary lists about 500,000 words, and there are a half-million technical and scientific terms still not catalogued?　英語が一番単語がある言語です。英語の辞書は５０万言葉があります。
- Three-quarters of the world's mail, telexes and cables are in English.　世界のメール、電子メールの三分の一は英語です。
- More than half of the world's technical and scientific periodicals are in English.　科学はジャーナルは半分以上は英語です。
- English is the medium for 80% of the information stored in the world's computers.　８０パーセントのコンピューターデーターは英語です。
- English is the language of navigation, aviation and of Christianity; it is the ecumenical language of the World Council of Churches.　航海や飛行は英語を使う。
- Five of the largest broadcasting companies in the world (CBS, NBC, ABC, BBC and CBC) transmit in English, reaching millions and millions of people all over the world.　世界五つのニュース会社は英語でレポートします。

Why study English? 何で英語を勉強する？

- You can enjoy travel almost anywhere in the world.　旅行したらどこでもコミューにケーソンができます。
- You can have access to the world's leading research and latest information.　一番新しい研究や一番新しい情報が読めます。
- You can have better career opportunities.　英語が話せるとカーリアの可能が多いです。

 **Try it. 何で英語が必要？**

1.
2.
3.

One with English コミュニケーションコース　Stage 0

My foundation 基盤を作ろう

Classroom Expressions 教室の表現

Please memorize these English classroom expressions.
この英語の表現を暗記してください。

English	Japanese
I have a question.	質問があります
Please say that again.	もう一度を言ってください
Please say that slowly	ゆっくり言ってください
Do you understand?	分かりますか？
I don't understand.	分かりません
I don't know.	知りません
Please wait	ちょっと待ってください。
How do you say _____ in English?	_____は英語で何と言いますか？
Please repeat after me.	繰り返してください
Please listen.	聞いてください
Please look.	見てください
Please say it in English.	英語で言ってください
Please pair up with a classmate.	ペアを作ってください
Good Job!	よくできました
Please	お願いします
_____ please.	___をください
Thank you	ありがとう
Find a partner	パートナーを見つけて
Make groups	グループを作って
Please be quiet	静かになって

Stage 0 — One with English コミュニケーションコ

My foundation 基盤を作ろう
The Alphabet

A	B	C	D	E	F
G	H	I	J	K	L
M	N	O	P	Q	R
S	T	U	V	W	X
Y	Z				

a	b	c	d	e	f
g	h	i	j	k	l
m	n	o	p	q	r
s	t	u	v	w	x
y	z				

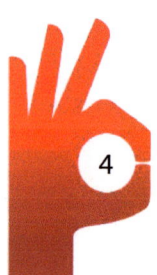

One with English コミュニケーションコース Stage 0

My foundation 基盤を作ろう

Romaji Chart

あ	い	う	え	お									ヴ
a	i	u	e	o									vu
か	き	く	け	こ	きゃ	きゅ	きょ	が	ぎ	ぐ	げ	ご	ぎゃ	ぎゅ	ぎょ
ka	ki	ku	ke	ko	kya	kyu	kyo	ga	gi	gu	ge	go	gya	gyu	gyo
さ	し	す	せ	そ	しゃ	しゅ	しょ	ざ	じ	ず	ぜ	ぞ	じゃ	じゅ	じょ
sa	shi	su	se	so	sha	shu	sho	za	ji	zu	ze	zo	jya	jyu	jyo
た	ち	つ	て	と	ちゃ	ちゅ	ちょ	だ	ぢ	づ	で	ど	ぢゃ	ぢゅ	ぢょ
ta	chi	tsu	te	to	cha	chu	cho	da	ji	zu	de	do	jya	jyu	jyo
な	に	ぬ	ね	の	にゃ	にゅ	にょ								
na	ni	nu	ne	no	nya	nyu	nyo								
は	ひ	ふ	へ	ほ	ひゃ	ひゅ	ひょ	ば	び	ぶ	べ	ぼ	びゃ	びゅ	びょ
ha	hi	fu	he	ho	hya	hyu	hyo	ba	bi	bu	be	bo	bya	byu	byo
								ぱ	ぴ	ぷ	ぺ	ぽ			
								pa	pi	pu	pe	po			
ま	み	む	め	も	みゃ	みゅ	みょ								
ma	mi	mu	me	mo	mya	myu	myo								
や		ゆ		よ											
ya		yu		yo											
ら	り	る	れ	ろ	りゃ	りゅ	りょ								
ra	ri	ru	re	ro	rya	ryu	ryo								
わ		を		ん											
wa		o		n											

Common Mistakes

このローマ字はコンピューターを入力したらひらがなかカタカナができますけどそのままでローマ字で英語喋る人にとして不全です。

×	○	×	○	×	×	○	×	○	×	○
sa	sha	ta	cha	da	ja	za	ha	fa	ra	la
si	shi	ti	chi	di	ji	zi	hi	fi	ri	li
su	shu	tu	chu	du	ju	zu	hu	fu	ru	lu
se	she	te	che	de	je	ze	he	fe	re	le
so	sho	to	cho	do	jo	zo	ho	fo	ro	lo

Stage 0 — One with English コミュニケーションコ

My foundation 基盤を作ろう

Capitalization 大文字

Proper nouns are name of specific people, palaces, or things. My name Eric is capitalzed because my name represents me and I am a unique individual. We can't capitalize "boy" or "girl" because they don't refer to a specific person.

固有名詞は特別な人か場所かものなど。私の名前「Eric」は私についての名詞と私は一人だけがいます。「boy」か「girl」は小文字ですから誰でもについて話せます。

Proper Nouns　固有名詞	
people's names 人の名前	Matsui Hideki, President Obama
names of places 場所の名前	Tokyo Dome, Chicago, Harvard University
brand names ブランド	Channel, Adidas, PlayStation
company names 会社の名前	Toyota, Boeing, Lawson
countries 国	Japan, America, Ireland
languages 言語	Japanese, English, Irish

My foundation 基盤を作ろう

One with English コミュニケーションコース　Stage 0

words 言葉

- **adverb 副詞**
  - always
  - sometimes
- **adjective 形容詞**
  - easy
  - soft
- **preposition 前置詞**
  - at
  - in
- **noun 名詞**
- **verb 動詞**

noun 名詞

singular 単数形
- snake
- baby
- potato

plural 複数形
- snakes
- babies
- potatoes

countable 可算
- dog
- city
- word

uncountable 不可算
- air
- water
- love

verb 動詞

be
- am
- is
- are

Infinitive 不定詞
- (to) fly
- (to) catch
- (to) play

regular 規則動詞
- work, worked, worked
- play, played, played
- move, moved, moved

Irregular 不規則動詞
- write, wrote, written
- catch, caught, caught
- fly, flew, flown

Present simple 現在形
- I play baseball.
- We study English.
- Do you like spagetti?

Past simple 過去形
- I went home.
- Eric wrote a book.
- We caught some fish.

Present perfect 現在完了
- I have been to China.
- We have sat here for hours.
- Has Eric seen that movie?

Past participle 過去分詞
- She hasn't finished yet.
- He had eaten too much.
- Eric hadn't been there before.

Present continuos 現在進行形
- I am eating dinner.
- Eric is living in Japan.
- Are they talking on the phone?

Past continuos 過去進行形
- We were having a good time.
- She was cooking breakfast.
- Were they crying?

Future 未来形
- They're going to walk home.
- Eric will eat sushi tonight.
- Are you going to excersise tomorrow?

Third person 三人称
- He plays tennis.
- Eric studies Japanese.
- Does your finger hurt?

Stage 0 — One with English コミュニケーションコ

My foundation 基盤を作ろう

 **Try it. Translate to English.**

例	英語で言ってください	Please say it in English.
1.	質問があります	
2.	知りません	
3.	繰り返してください	
4.	パートナーを見つけて	
5.	ちょっと待ってください。	

 **Try it. ローマ字で書いて.**

例	ローマ字・ふりがな	Alphabet
1.	カタカナ	
2.	しんたろ	
3.	しゃぶしゃぶ	
4.	けんどう	
5.	いちろ すずき	

✅ **Try it. Choose an answer.**

1.	つなみ	○ a. tunami	○ b. tsunami	○ c. dunami
2.	英語	○ a. English	○ b. eigo	○ c. english
3.	カラオケ	○ a. karaoke	○ b. kariyoke	○ c. Karaoke
4.	すし	○ a. suushi	○ b. Sushi	○ c. sushi
5.	大阪	○ a. Oosaka	○ b. Ohsaka	○ c. Osaka
6.	べんとう	○ a. bentou	○ b. Bentou	○ c. bento
7.	木村　卓也	○ a. Kimutaku	○ b. Kimura Takuya	○ c. Kimura takuya
8.	枝豆	○ a. Edamame	○ b. eda mame	○ c. edamame
9.	横浜	○ a. Youkohama	○ b. Yoko Hama	○ c. Yokohama
10.	ソニ	○ a. Soni	○ b. Sony	○ c. Souny
11.	富士山	○ a. mt. fuji	○ b. Mt. fuji	○ c. Mt. Fuji
12.	リサ	○ a. Risa	○ b. Lisa	○ c. risa

One with English コミュニケーションコース — Stage 0

My foundation 基盤を作ろう

Challenge!

Write as many in each category in the given time. (1~5 minutes)
1~5分でできるだけで言葉を書きましょう。

Nouns 名詞	apple, Eric, winter, …
Verbs 動詞	study, push, consider, …
Adjectives 形容詞	small, expensive, smart, …

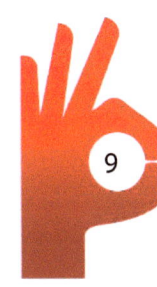

Stage 0　One with English コミュニケーションⅠ

My foundation 基盤を作ろう

One with English コミュニケーションコース　Stage 1

My Self Introduction 私の自己紹介

テーマ：	Theme:
自己紹介	Self-Introduction
毎日の挨拶	Everyday Greetings
Hi, I'm Eric. Nice to meet you. *How are you? I'm OK, and you?*	
文法：	Grammar:
不定冠詞	Indefinite Articles
I'm **a** teacher. I'm **an** office worker.	
BE 動詞	Be Verbs
am, is , are	
国籍の接尾辞	Nationality suffixes
Americ**an**, Ir**ish**, Japan**ese**, Brazil**ian**	
単語	Vocabulary
国	Countries
国籍	Nationalities
番号１〜９９	Numbers 1-99

Stage 1 — One with English コミュニケーションコース
My Self Introduction 私の自己紹介
Stage 1 - Level 1 – "The first meeting"

A: Hello, I'm Eric Hawkinson. I'm from Arizona. I'm American. How about you?

B: Hello, I'm Yumi Takamoto. I'm from Kyoto. I'm Japanese. I'm a student. And you?

A: No, I'm not. I'm an instructor. Nice to meet you, Ms. Takamoto.

B: Please call me Yumi. Nice to meet you, too!

A: Eric
B: Yumi

Vocabulary:

単語	意味	単語	意味	単語	意味
I	わたしは	am	です	nice	よい
to	へ	meet	出会う	you	あなたは
too	もまた	may	していいか？	call	呼ぶ
please	お願い	call	呼ぶ	me	私

Cultural Point

　日本では自己紹介する時名字使います。外国では名前かあだ名を使います。その場合はよく日本人は丁寧に言いたいので「Mr./Mrs.」をつける傾向があります。Mr./Mrs.は名前とあだ名には合いません。名字か名前のどちらで呼んでよい分からない場合は「**May I call you ... ?**（...と呼んでよろしいですか？）」を使えばいいです。

　日本ではじめて出会う人と話す時に何の情報を交換しますか？日本ではよく最初の質問は年齢についてですが外国では失礼です。外国では仕事についての質問が多いです。その他に出身や興味などの質問もよいでしょう。

One with English コミュニケーションコース　Stage 1

My Self Introduction 私の自己紹介

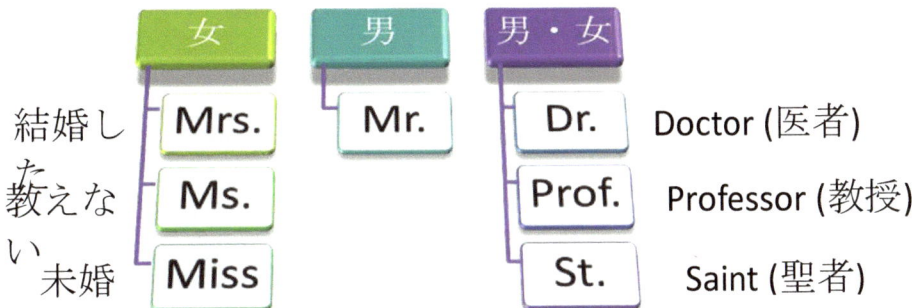

Mr./Mrs./Ms./Miss

(例) Mr. Hawkinson
使う時：相手があまり分からない人や年上

First name (名前)

(例) Eric
使う時：相手が友達や同級生

Nickname (あだな)

(例) "Hawk","Big man"
使う時：相手の頼みで

Using Titles

When using a title like Mr. or Mrs. you must pair it with a last name and never a first name unless requested.
MR. や MRS. を使う時に名字を使わなければならない。

Let's write!

Hello.
My name is _____.
　　　　　順番は1．名前　－＞2．名字

Please call me _____.
　　　　　名前か MR./MRS./MS.＋名字かあだな

Nice to meet you.

Let's chat!

A: Hello. My name is (名前＋名字). What's your name?
B: Hello (Mr./Ms.+相手の名字). I'm (名前＋名字). Please call me (名前か Mr./Ms.+名字かあだな).
A: Nice to meet you, (相手の頼んだ名)
B: Nice to meet you, too!

Stage 1 — One with English コミュニケーションコース

My Self Introduction 私の自己紹介

Introducing yourself: はじめてのあいさつ

Phrase 表現	Alternative 他の言い方	Meaning 意味
Can I introduce myself?	May I introduce myself?	自己紹介していいか？
My name is ...	My name's ...	私の名前は...
I'm ...	I am ...	私は...
I don't think we've met.		まだ会ったことないと思います。

Phrase 表現	Meaning 意味	Reply 返事	Meaning 返事の意味
Excuse me, are you ...?	すみません。あなたは（名前）ですか？	No. I'm ...	違います。私は...
You must be ...	あなたは...だろうね。	Yes, that's right.	はい、そうです。
You are ..., aren't you?	あなたは...ですね。		
Have we met?	私たちは会いましたか？	No. I'm ... / Yes, we have.	まだですね。私は... / はい、会いました。
How do you do?	はじめまして	How do you do?	はじめまして
Nice to meet you.	はじめまして	Nice to meet you, too.	はじめまして
Please, call me ...	私を...と呼んでください。	Nice to meet you, ...	（名前）、はじめまして
I'm glad to meet you.	はじめまして	Glad to meet you, too.	はじめまして

Introducing someone else: 友達の紹介

Phrase 表現	Alternative 他の言い方	Meaning 意味
I'd like you to meet ...	I want you to meet ...	...を紹介したいです。
Have you met ... ?		...をお会いましたか？
This is ...		こちらは...

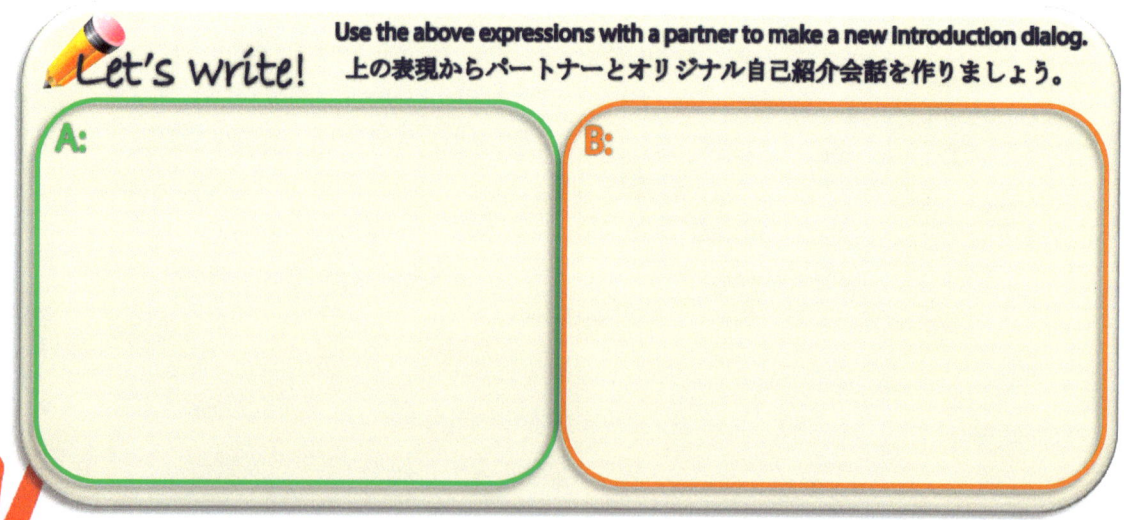

Let's write! Use the above expressions with a partner to make a new introduction dialog.
上の表現からパートナーとオリジナル自己紹介会話を作りましょう。

A:

B:

My Self Introduction 私の自己紹介
Toolbox – "The first meeting"

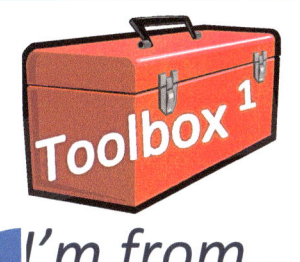

Toolbox 1 — I'm from ...

私は…出身です。/ 私は…からきました。

Canada	カナダ	America	アメリカ
Japan	日本	China	中国
Korea	韓国	Ireland	アイルランド
Australia	オーストラリア	Thailand	タイ

国＋an, ian, ese, ish

Toolbox 2 — I'm ...

私は…人です。

Canadian	カナダ人	American	アメリカ人
Japanese	日本人	Chinese	中国人
Korean	韓国人	Irish	アイルランド人
Australian	オーストラリア人	*Thai	タイ人

✓ Try it. Choose an answer.

1. Brazil (ブラジル)　　○ a. Brazilese　　○ b. Brazilan　　○ c. Brazilian
2. India (インド)　　○ a. Indese　　○ b. Indian　　○ c. Indish
3. Italy (イタリア)　　○ a. Italese　　○ b. Italian　　○ c. Italish
4. Spain (スペイン)　　○ a. Spainese　　○ b. Spainian　　○ c. Spanish
5. Turkey (トルコ)　　○ a. Trukese　　○ b. Turkian　　○ c. Turkish
6. Vietnam (ベトナム)　　○ a. Vietnamese　　○ b. Vietnamish　　○ c. Vietnamian
7. Mexico (メキシコ)　　○ a. Mexican　　○ b. Mexese　　○ c. Mexish

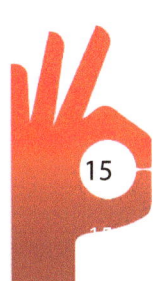

Stage 1 One with English コミュニケーションコース

My Self Introduction 私の自己紹介

A / AN は「一つの」意味する。

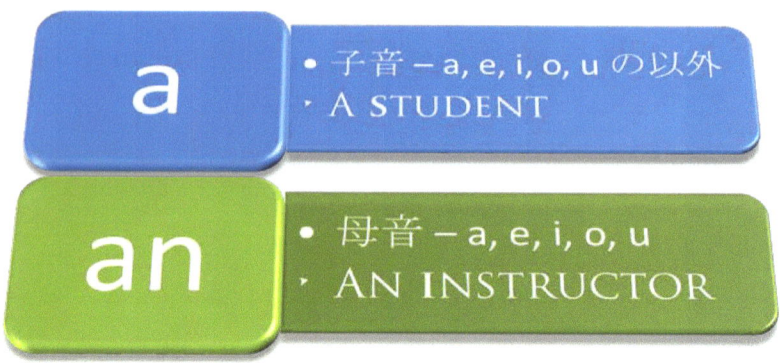

- 子音 – a, e, i, o, u の以外
- A STUDENT

- 母音 – a, e, i, o, u
- AN INSTRUCTOR

When we think of one non-specific item we put "a" or "an" in front of that noun. When we have a specific item in mind we use "the".

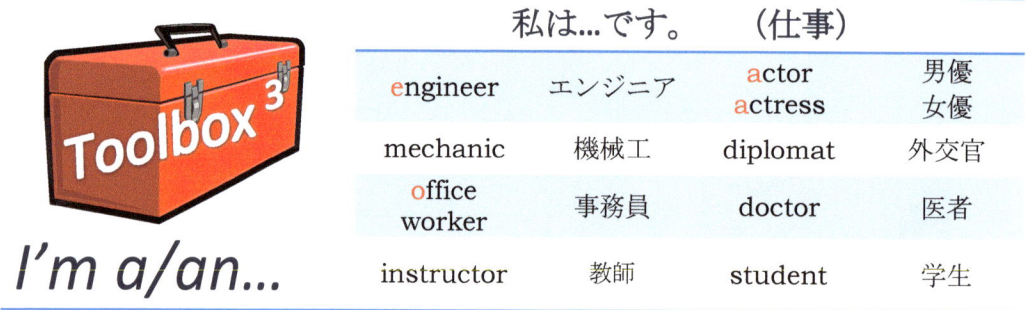

I'm a/an...

	私は…です。		（仕事）
engineer	エンジニア	actor / actress	男優 / 女優
mechanic	機械工	diplomat	外交官
office worker	事務員	doctor	医者
instructor	教師	student	学生

Let's chat!

Hello. I'm ___名前___.
I'm from ___出身___.
And you?
I'm ___国籍___.
How about you?
I'm a/an ___仕事___.
And you?
Nice to meet you.

Hi. I'm ___名前___.
I'm from ___出身___.
I'm ___国籍___.
I'm a/an ___仕事___.
Nice to meet you, too.

One with English コミュニケーションコース Stage 1

My Self Introduction 私の自己紹介

Dialog 1 – "Daily greetings"

Hello

Hi

How are you?

I'm fine. And you?

I'm great!

See you later.

See you!

Vocabulary:

単語	意味	単語	意味	単語	意味
hi	こんにちは	hello	こんにちは	how	どう
are	です	fine	良い	see	見る
later	後	and	と	great	すばらしい

"How are you?"の返事で自分の気持ちを表してみよう。

Toolbox 1 How are you? の返事 I'm...	(How are you?の返事)		/ 私は…です。	
	great	すばらしい	fine	良い
	so so	まあまあ	OK	オッケー
	not good	良くない	terrible	最低

← 良い   良くない →

great   fine   OK   so so   not good   terrible

Stage 1 — One with English コミュニケーションコース

My Self Introduction 私の自己紹介

Greetings: あいさつ

Word 単語	Alternative 他の言い方	Meaning 意味
Hello	Hi	こんにちは
Good morning		おはよう
Good afternoon		こんにちは
Good evening		こんばんは
Good to see you	Nice to see you	会えてよかった

Pleasantries: 毎日の質問

Phrase 表現	Meaning 意味	Reply 返事	Meaning 返事の意味
How are you?	元気？	Fine, thanks. And you?	元気よ。あなたは？
How have you been?	最近はどう？	Very well. And you?	いいよ。あなたは？
What's up?	調子はどう？	Not much. And you?	あまりない。あなたは？
How is your boyfriend?	彼はどう？	He's fine.	彼は元気です。
How is your girlfriend?	彼女はどう？	She's fine.	彼女は元気です。
How is your family?	家族はどう？	They're fine.	家族は元気です。

Naturally Speaking

Formal / Business 形だけのあいさつ	Informal / Friendly 打ち解けた	
Hello	Hey / Hi / Yo / Hiya	
How are you?	How are you doing?	Fine, and you?
	How are ya?	Not bad.
	What's up?	Not much.
	How's it goin'?	Not bad.
Goodbye	Bye / See you / See you later / See ya / Later	
Yes	Yeah / Yep / Uh-huh	
No	Nope / Nah / Uh-uh	

My Self Introduction 私の自己紹介

Good-byes: さようなら

Phrase 表現	Alternative 他の言い方	Meaning 意味
Good bye	Bye	さようなら
See you later	Later	では、またあとでね
See you soon	See ya	また
I must go now	Gotta go	失礼します/行かなきゃいけない

Pleasantries: フレンドリーな表現

Phrase 表現	Meaning 意味	Reply 返事	Meaning 返事の意味
Have a nice day.	良い一日を	Same to you.	あなたも
Have a nice weekend.	良い週末を	Thanks. You too.	どうも。あなたも
Have a nice trip.	良い旅行を	Thank you.	ありがとう
Have a nice afternoon.	良い昼を	Thanks.	どうも
Have a nice evening.	良い夜を	You do the same.	あなたも

To next time: 今度を楽しみしている

Phrase 表現	Meaning 意味	Reply 返事	Meaning 返事の意味
I hope to see you again.	また会いたい	I hope so, too.	私も希望する
See you on the 13th.	また１３日に	See you then.	それで
I look forward to …	…に楽しみしている	Me too.	私も。

See you in/on/at …

Term (術語)	use (使う時)	Example (例)
on	Date / 日付	See you *on* January 13th.
	Day of the week / 曜日	See you *on* Wednesday.
in	Month / 月	See you *in* May.
	Year / 年	See you *in* 2012.
at	Time / 時間	See you *at* 3:30.
	Place / 場所	See you *at* school.
next	Unspecific times はっきり決まってない時	See you *next* week.
	The next day, week, or year 次の	See you *next* time.

Stage 1 One with English コミュニケーションコース

My Self Introduction 私の自己紹介

Reading Stage 1 – My Profile

Nicebook

Home   Profile   Account

Profile Picture

First name: Eric
Middle name: Charles
Last name: Hawkinson
Nickname: Tidehawk

My Profile

Hometown: Tucson, Arizona
Nationality: USA
Birthday: September 9th
Likes: cheese, languages, basketball, and computers
Hobbies: playing sports, surfing the internet

About me:
  Hello. May I introduce myself? My name is Eric Charles Hawkinson. Please call me Eric. I am from Arizona. I am American. I am a teacher in Japan. I am also a basketball player and a gamer. I have one younger brother back in Arizona. My favorite food is cheese and my favorite subject is astronomy.

I'm very glad to meet you.
Have a nice day!

True or False
1. Eric is from Alaska.   T   F
2. Eric likes cheese.   T   F
3. Eric is a student.   T   F
4. Eric lives in Japan.   T   F
5. Eric has two brothers.   T   F

Answer the questions.
6. What is Eric's nickname?

7. Where is Eric from?

8. What is Eric's favorite food?

One with English コミュニケーションコース　Stage 1

My Self Introduction 私の自己紹介
Write your own profile.
自分のプロフィールを書きましょう。

Nicebook

My Profile

Hometown:
Nationality:
Birthday:
Likes:

Hobbies:

About me:

My Self Introduction 私の自己紹介

A. 下線のところに合う英語を書きましょう。

1. E = Eric Hawkinson, J = Jun
    J: Excuse me, _____ Eric Hawkinson?
    E: Yes, that's _____.
    J: May I _____ myself?
         I'm Jun. How do you do?
    E: _____, Jun.

2. M = Michael Jordan, L = Larry Bird
    L: You _____ be Mr. Jordan.
    M: Yes. Please _____ me Michael.
    L: I'm Larry.
         I'm _____ basketball player, too.
    M: Nice to _____ you, Larry.
    L: Nice to meet you, _____.

3. Y = Yumi, K = Keiko, A = Akio
    Y: Keiko! Good to see you again. _____ are things?
    K: Hello, Yumi. I'm fine, thanks. I'd like you to _____ Akio.
    Y: Nice to meet you, Akio.
    A: Nice to meet you, _____.

B. 正しい答えに○してください。

4. I'm (a / an / 無し) teacher.
5. I'm (a / an / 無し) firefighter.
6. I'm (a / an / 無し) Mr. Hawkinson.
7. I'm (a / an / 無し) announcer.
8. I'm (a / an / 無し) pilot.
9. I'm (a / an / 無し) Eric.
10. I'm (a / an / 無し) student.

One with English コミュニケーションコース　Stage 1

My Self Introduction 私の自己紹介

B. この表現に合う返事を書きましょう。

11. How are you?
　　_____

12. How do you do?
　　_____

13. Pleased to meet you.
　　_____

14. It was nice meeting you.
　　_____

15. See you next week.
　　_____

16. Have we met?
　　_____

C. 正しい答えに〇してください。

17. See you (**on / in / at / next**) Saturday.
18. See you (**on / in / at / next**) week.
19. See you (**on / in / at / next**) February 14th.
20. See you (**on / in / at / next**) 3 o'clock.
21. See you (**on / in / at / next**) year.
22. See you (**on / in / at / next**) school.

Stage 1 — One with English コミュニケーションコース

My Self Introduction 私の自己紹介

Please fill in the country names and nationalities.
国の名前と国籍を書いてください。

#	Flag 旗	Country 国	Nationality 国籍
1.	🇨🇳		
2.	✚		
3.	🇰🇷		
4.	🇧🇷		
5.	🇿🇦		
6.	🇪🇸		
7.	🇳🇴		
8.	🇺🇸		
9.			
10.	🇲🇽		
11.			
12.	🇻🇳		
13.	🇫🇷		
14.	🇮🇳		

Country list

中国 China	ブラジル Brazil	南アフリカ South Africa	イギリス England	ベトナム Viet Nam	メキシコ Mexico	フランス France
タイ Thailand	ノルウェー Norway	スペイン Spain	アメリカ America	ロシア Russia	韓国 Korea	インド India

One with English コミュニケーションコース Stage 2
My First Chat - 私の最初チャット

STAGE TWO

My First Chat
私の最初のチャット

テーマ：	Theme:
所有, 簡単な疑問文	Yes/No Questions, Possession
文法：	**Grammar:**
これ/これらはなに？ どこにありますか Be 動詞 所有代名詞	What *is this/are these*? Where *is/are* … ? Be Verbs Possessive adjectives

Stage 2 — One with English コミュニケーションコース
My First Chat 私の最初のチャット

Vocabulary:

単語	意味	単語	意味	単語	意味
am	です	I	私	drummer	ドラマー
is	いる	he	彼	guitarist	ギター奏者
are	ある	she	彼女	singer	歌手
		we	私たち	band	バンド

One with English コミュニケーションコース　Stage 2

My First Chat - 私の最初チャット

Let's Talk Circle game

How to play	やり方
The first person gives a short self-introduction. 　Hi. I am Eric. I am from Arizona. 　I am American. I am a teacher. The next person introduces the first person then introduces him/herself. Use He + is or She + is and use we + are if your information is the same. 　He is Eric. He is from Arizona. 　We are American. He is a teacher. 　I am Tom. I am … Each new person in the circle must introduce all the people that came before.	最初の人は英語で自己紹介をしてください。 例：Hi. I am Eric. I am from Arizona. 　　I am American. I am a teacher. 次の人は前の人を紹介してください、男の人だったら He is を使って女の人だったら She is を使って、同じ出身や国籍の場合は We are を使ってください。 例：He is Eric. He is from Arizona. 　　We are American. He is a teacher. 　　I am Tom. I am … 進んだらどんどん紹介をする人数が増えていきます。ファイト！
Stage 2	**ステージ　2**
Repeat the game. This time use contractions for the be verbs.	もう一回しましょう。今回は主語＋Be 動詞の縮約を使いましょう。

Contractions for Be Verbs. Be 動詞の縮約

Stage 2　One with English コミュニケーションコース

My First Chat 私の最初のチャット

Dialog – "Asking questions"

Are you from China?

No, I'm not. I'm from Japan.

Are you a teacher?

Yes, I am.

Vocabulary:

単語	意味	単語	意味	単語	意味
are	です	no	いいえ	yes	はい
I	私は	am	です	from	…から
you	あなたは	I'm	(I am)	not	ではない

is, am, are を be 動詞といいます。
日本語にすると「〜です。」「〜いる（ある）。」の２つの意味があり、文の中では述語になります。
主語(〜は、〜が) によって is, am, are を使い分けます。

> 例　**I am** from Kyoto.　わたしは京都出身です。
> 　　**We are** from Kyoto.　私たちは京都出身です。
> 　　**Jun is** from Kyoto.　ケンは京都出身です。

My First Chat - 私の最初チャット

is , am, are を be 動詞といいます。
日本語にすると「〜です。」「〜いる(ある)。」の2つの意味があり、文の中では**述語**になります。
主語(〜は、〜が) によって is, am, are を使い分けます。

> 例　　I **am** from Kyoto.　わたしは京都出身です。
> 　　　We **are** from Kyoto.　私たちは京都出身です。
> 　　　Jun **is** from Kyoto.　ケンは京都出身です。

代名詞	I	He, She, It, This, That 単数形	You, We, They 複数形
原型	be	be	be
現在形	am	is	are
過去形	was	was	were

be 動詞の疑問文

be 動詞の文を疑問文にするには be 動詞を文頭に出します。
普通の文（肯定文）　主語＋be 動詞＋・・・　　　　This is your book.
疑問文　　　　　　be 動詞＋主語＋・・・？　Is this your book?

答え方

Is this your book?　　　　　答　Yes, it is. /No, it's not.　物が主語のときは it を使う
Are you a teacher?　　　　答　Yes, I am. / No, I'm not.
　　　you できかれているので I で答える
Is Ken from Tokyo?　　　　答　Yes, he is. / No, he's not.
　　　男の人が主語なので he を使う
※be 動詞で聞かれているので be 動詞で答える。

Stage 2 — One with English コミュニケーションコース

My First Chat 私の最初のチャット

Toolbox – "The first meeting"

Toolbox 1 — Are you from …?

あなたは…出身ですか。

Canada	カナダ	America	アメリカ
Japan	日本	China	中国
Korea	韓国	Ireland	アイルランド
Australia	オーストラリア	Thailand	タイ

Toolbox 2 — Are you … ?

あなたは…人ですか。

Canadian	カナダ人	American	アメリカ人
Japanese	日本人	Chinese	中国人
Korean	韓国人	Irish	アイルランド人
Australian	オーストラリア人	Thai	タイ人

Toolbox 3 — Are you a/an… ?

あなたは…ですか。（仕事）

engineer	エンジニア	actor / actress	男優 / 女優
mechanic	機械工	diplomat	外交官
office worker	事務員	doctor	医者
instructor	教師	student	学生

Yes, I am. はい、そうです。　　**No, I'm not.** いいえ、違います。

My First Chat - 私の最初チャット

Dialog – "Asking questions 2"

- Is this your newspaper?
- No, it's not. It's his newspaper.
- Is that my pen you're using?
- Oh! Sorry. Yes, it is.

Vocabulary:

単語	意味	単語	意味	単語	意味
this	これ	It's	It is	my	私の
that	それ、あれ	you're	You are	his	かれの
sorry	ごめん	your	あなたの	newspaper	新聞

Answering Questions

質問	はい、そうです。	いいえ、違います。
Is this/that … ?	Yes, it is.	No, it is not. No, it's not. No, it isn't
Are you … ?	Yes, I am.	No, I am not. No, I'm not.
Is he/she … ?	Yes, he/she is.	No, he/she is not. No, he's/she's not. No, he/she isn't.
Am I … ?	Yes, you are.	No, you are not. No, you're not. No, you aren't.
Are we … ?	Yes, we are.	No, we are not. No, we're not. No, we aren't.

Stage 2   One with English コミュニケーションコース

My First Chat 私の最初のチャット

Dialog – "Are these/those?"

Are these your video games?
Yes, they are. They are very fun.
Are those your comics?
No, they aren't. They are my friend's.

Vocabulary:

単語	意味	単語	意味	単語	意味
these	これら	is	単数形の BE 動詞	very	とても
those	それら	are	複数形の BE 動詞	comic	まんが
fun	楽しい	they	かれら	video game	テレビゲーム

Answering Questions

質問	はい、そうです。	いいえ、違います。
Are these … ? Are those … ?	Yes, they are.	No, they are not. No, they're not. No, they aren't.

One with English コミュニケーションコース　Stage 2

My First Chat - 私の最初チャット

Toolbox – "Is this your newspaper?"

所有代名詞
Possessive adjectives

私の	my
彼の	his
彼女の	her
あなたの	your
私たちの	our
彼たちの	their
エリックの	Eric's
誰の	whose

Is this/that ...? Are these/those ...?
これ/それ/これら/それらは ...（誰のもの）...ですか？

ある・いる	これ/それ これら/それら	誰の		もの
Is	this これ that それ	my your his her	私の あなたの 彼の 彼女の	single object 単数形のもの
Are	these これら those それら	it's Eric's everyone's nobody's	何かの エリックの みんなの 誰もないの	multiple objects 複数形のもの

Is this/that ...? Are these/those ...?
これ/それ/あれは ...（誰の関係ない）...ですか？

ある・いる	これ/それ これら/それら	誰の		もの
Is	this これ that それ	a / an the 無し	一つの 特定の 固有名詞 の場合	single object 単数形のもの
Are	these これら those それら	a couple a few some 無し	二つの 三つの いくつかの 数えない	multiple objects 複数形のもの

Stage 2   One with English コミュニケーションコース

My First Chat 私の最初のチャット

例：This is my iPhone.

These are my coins.

How to play	やり方
Choose one of your cards and put it into your pocket or hide it in your hand. Next make a sentence about the card. You can either make a true statement or you can make a lie. 例：**This is a book.** Your partner has to decide whether or not your is lying. If you think your partner is lying say **"NO WAY!"** and if your think your partner is telling the truth say **"I believe you"**. If your partner is correct in choosing if it was a lie or the truth you must give that card to your partner. If your partner was fooled he/she must give you a card. The person with the most cards at the end wins.	一つのカードを選んでポケットに入れてください。パートナーにカードについて文書を言ってください。その文書はうそでもいいです。 例：　This is a book. 相手はうそと思ったら**"NO WAY!"**を言って、本当と思ったら**"I believe you"**を言ってください。 正しいかったらカードを渡さなければいけない。だまされたの場合はカードをもらいます。 時間が終わった時に一番多くカードが持っている人が勝ちです。
Stage 2	**ステージ　2**
Repeat the game. This time pretend all the items are in plural form. Ex. These are some books.	もう一回しましょう。今回はカードのものが複数形になります。　例：　These are some books.

Put it to practice

A. 正しいの BE 動詞を○してください。

肯定分　Affirmative Sentences
1. This (am / is / are) a desk.
2. That (am / is / are) my book.
3. These (am / is / are) his comics.
4. Those (am / is / are) your video games.
5. I (am / is / are) from Arizona.
6. You (am / is / are) my friend.
7. He (am / is / are) a teacher.
8. She (am / is / are) an actress.
9. They (am / is / are) students.
10. We (am / is / are) friends.

否定文　Negative Sentences
11. This (am not / isn't / aren't) a desk.
12. That (am not / isn't / aren't) my book.
13. These (am not / isn't / aren't) his comics.
14. Those (am not / isn't / aren't) your video games.
15. I (am not / isn't / aren't) from Arizona.
16. You (am not / isn't / aren't) my friend.
17. He (am not / isn't / aren't) a teacher.
18. She (am not / isn't / aren't) an actress.
19. They (am not / isn't / aren't) students.
20. We (am not / isn't / aren't) friends.

Stage 2 — One with English コミュニケーションコース

My First Chat 私の最初のチャット

Put it to practice

B. 正しい主語と BE 動詞を書いてください。

疑問文　Question Sentences

21. _____ a desk?
22. _____ my book?
23. _____ his comics?
24. _____ your video games?
25. _____ from Arizona?
26. _____ my friend?
27. _____ a teacher?
28. _____ an actress?
29. _____ students?
30. _____ friends?

C. ２１番から３０番までの質問の返事を書いてください。

31. Yes, _____.　　No, _____.
32. Yes, _____.　　No, _____.
33. Yes, _____.　　No, _____.
34. Yes, _____.　　No, _____.
35. Yes, _____.　　No, _____.
36. Yes, _____.　　No, _____.
37. Yes, _____.　　No, _____.
38. Yes, _____.　　No, _____.
39. Yes, _____.　　No, _____.
40. Yes, _____.　　No, _____.

One with English コミュニケーションコース　Stage 2

My First Chat - 私の最初チャット

Put it to practice

D. 英語に翻訳してください。

41. これは私のえんぴつです。
_____

42. それはあなたの新聞です。
_____

43. これは私たちの教室です。
_____

44. それらは彼たちのえんぴつです。
_____

45. それらはあなたの本ですか？
_____

46. これはエリックのコンピューターですか？
_____

47. 私たちは友達です。
_____

48. 私たちは友達ですか？　　はい、そうですよ。
_____

49. エリック先生はあなたの英語の先生ですか？
_____

50. 彼女はアメリカからやってきましたか？　いいえ、違います。
_____

Stage 2 — One with English コミュニケーションコース

My First Chat 私の最初のチャット

Read, read, read

Read the following descriptions of famous people. Can you guess who they are?

下に有名な人について文章が書いてあります。この人誰でしょうか？

1. He was born on December 5th, 1901 in Burbank, California. He was a film producer and founded his own company. The company he started is the biggest animation company in the world today. He created some of the world most well-known characters.	2. She is a famous actress. She is in many popular movies. She is the character Lara Croft in the movie Tomb Raider. She is a very beautiful woman. Her partner is Brad Pit.	3. They are a famous band in Japan. They are singers and actors. They have a popular cooking show in T.V. The members of this group are in many movies and television shows in Japan. They have 4 members in the group.
Who is he?	Who is she?	Who are they?

Write, write, write

Think of a famous person or group. Write some hints about him/her/them.
有名な人を考えましょう。その人についてヒントをかきましょう。正しく BE 動詞を使いましょう。

One with English コミュニケーションコース　Stage 3

My Room 私の部屋

STAGE THREE
My Room 私の部屋

テーマ：	Theme:
私の部屋 忘れ物、置くもの	Lost items, Placed items Describing your room
文法：	Grammar:
複数形 どこにありますか 所有代名詞	Plural nouns Where *is/are* ...? Possessive adjectives

Stage 3 — One with English コミュニケーションコース
My Room 私の部屋

- What's this?
- It's a mint candy.
- What are these?
- They are some chocolate candies.
- Can I have some?
- Sure. One or two?
- Just one candy please.

Vocabulary:

単語	意味	単語	意味	単語	意味
What's	What is	it's	it is	mint	ミント
this	これ	sure	もちろん	chocolate	チョコー
these	それら	candy	キャンディ	just	だけ
some	いくつか	candies	candyの複数形	Can I have …	…もらいますか？

noun/名詞	singular/単数形	plural/複数形
本	book	book**s**
箱	box	box**es**
人	person	people

My Room 私の部屋

Spelling – つづり方

noun/名詞	singular/単数形	plural/複数形
Most nouns become plural simply by adding an "s"	*大部分の名詞は「s」をつけたら複数形になります。*	
本	book	book**s**
Words that end with o, sh, ch, x, and s sounds are made plural with "es"	*o, sh, ch, x, s で終わる言葉は「es」をつけます。*	
箱	box	box**es**
じゃがいも	potato	potato**es**
There are many special cases	*特別の複数形が多いのです。*	
人	person	people
子供	child	children
Consonant + y ends in "ies"	*子音＋y の終わりことばは「ies」*	
キャンディ	candy	cand**ies**
赤ちゃん	baby	bab**ies**
Sometimes the plural and singular are the same	*単数形と複数形は同じこともあります。*	
魚	fish	fish
鹿	deer	deer

Pronunciation – 発音

/s/		/z/		/iz/	
言葉の最後の発音	例	言葉の最後の発音	例	言葉の最後の発音	例
/k/ [k]	cooks	/d/ [d]	cards	/s/ [s]	races
/f/ [f]	cliffs	/b/ [b]	crabs	/z/ [z]	pauses
/p/ [p]	cups	/g/ [g]	rugs	/sh/ [ʃ]	wishes
/t/ [t]	hats	/l/ [l]	deals	/ch/ [tʃ]	churches
/th/ [θ]	myths	/m/ [m]	plums	/zh/ [ʒ]	judges
		/n/ [n]	fans	/dz/ [dʒ]	ages
		/ng/ [ŋ]	kings		
		/r/ [r]	tears		

Stage 3 — One with English コミュニケーションコース
My Room 私の部屋

Dialog 1 – "Lost Items"

- Where is my bag?
- It's by the desk.
- Where is your passport?
- It's in my pocket.
- Good.
- Where are our plane tickets?
- They are on the table.

Vocabulary:

単語	意味	単語	意味	単語	意味
Where	どこ	my	私の	your	あなたの
our	私たちの	on	〜の上	in	〜の中
by	〜のとなり	table	テーブル	pocket	ポケット
It's		ticket	きっぷ	passport	パースポート

どこですか。〜の上、〜の中、〜の下、〜のとなり

on　in　under　by

My Room 私の部屋

Finding lost items: 忘れ物を探す時

Phrase 表現	Alternative 他の言い方	Meaning 意味
Where is my … ?		私の…はどこですか。
Have you seen my … ?		私の…を見ましたか。
Has anyone found my … ?		だれか…を見つかれましたか。
Excuse me, I've lost my …		すみません、私の…がなくなった

Found items: 忘れ物を見つかった時

Phrase 表現	Alternative 他の言い方	Meaning 意味
Excuse me, is this your …?		すみません、これはあなたの…ですか。
I found this.		これは見つかったです。
Someone left this.		だれかこれを忘れた。
This was left …		これは（場所）にありました。
Please put this in the lost and found.		これは遺失物取扱所に渡してください。

Returning items: 忘れ物を渡す時

Phrase 表現	Meaning 意味	Reply 返事	Meaning 返事の意味
I think you left this.	あなたはこれを忘れたと思います。	Oh yes! Thank you!	そうです。ありがとう！
		That is not mine, sorry.	私のではないです。
Excuse me, is this yours?	すみません。これはあなたのですか。	Oh yes! Thank you!	そうです。ありがとう！
		It's not mine, sorry.	私のではないです。
You forgot this.	あなたはこれを忘れました。	You're right! Thank you!	そうです。ありがとう！
		Oh that was already there.	あぁ、それは前からあったです。

Toolbox – "Where is it?"

Stage 3 — One with English コミュニケーションコース
My Room 私の部屋

Where is my bag? It's by the desk.

Let's ask!

Where is (someone's) (item)?
(だれの)(もの)はどこですか。

どこ	です	だれの		もの
Where	is 単数形	my your our their his her Eric's the 無し	私の あなたの 私たちの あなたたちの 彼の 彼女の エリックの (だれの関係ないの場合) (人を探し場合)	(Object) (もの) (Person) (人の名前)
	are 複数形			

Let's answer!

(もの)(人)		です	～の上、下、中、となり	だれの	場所、もの
It	もの(単数形)	is	on	my	場所、もの
He	彼			your	
She	彼女		in	our	
Eric	(人の名前)			their	
They	彼たち もの(複数形)	are	under	his her	
We	私たち		by	Eric's the	

My Room 私の部屋

Stage 3

Bedroom items:

単語	意味	単語	意味	単語	意味
wall	かべ	window	窓	desk	机
box	箱	chair	いす	shelf	本棚

A

Dialog:

Q. Where (is/are) the … ?

A. (It's, They're) (on, in, under, by) the …

*(He/She is …)

{#}単語	意味	{#}単語	意味	{#}単語	意味
1. clock	時計	2. CDs	CD	3. computer	パソコン
4. picture	絵	5. trash can	ゴミ箱	6. comics	まんが
7. CD player	CDプレーヤー	8. guitar	ギター	9. pencils	えんぴつ
10. cup	カップ	11. Jun	じゅん	12. Eric	エリック

Stage 3 — One with English コミュニケーションコース

My Room 私の部屋

Bedroom items:

単語	意味	単語	意味	単語	意味
wall	かべ	window	窓	desk	机
box	箱	chair	いす	shelf	本棚

Dialog:

Q. Where (is/are) the … ?

A. (It's, They're) (on, in, under, by) the …

*(He/She is …)

{#} 単語	意味	{#} 単語	意味	{#} 単語	意味
1. clock	時計	2. CDs	CD	3. computer	パソコン
4. picture	絵	5. trash can	ゴミ箱	6. comics	まんが
7. CD player	CDプレーヤー	8. guitar	ギター	9. pencils	えんぴつ
10. cup	カップ	11. Jun	じゅん	12. Eric	エリック

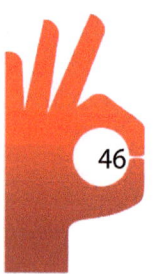

My Room 私の部屋

Dialog 1 – "Placement"

- Here is some ice cream for you.
- Really? Thanks.
- Vanilla is on the bottom.
- What's on top?
- Chocolate is on top.
- What's in the middle?
- Strawberry is in the middle.

Vocabulary:

単語	意味	単語	意味	単語	意味
top	一番上	bottom	一番下	middle	間中
vanilla	バニラ	chocolate	チョコ	strawberry	イチゴ
ice cream	アイスクリーム	here	ここ	for	…のため
really?	本当に？	thanks	どうも	what	何

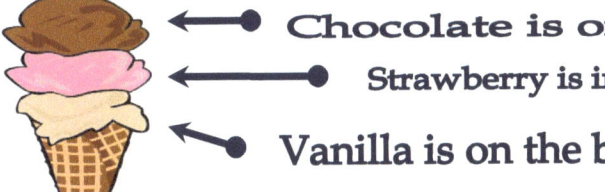

On top, in the middle, and on the bottom

- Chocolate is on top.
- Strawberry is in the middle
- Vanilla is on the bottom

Stage 3 — One with English コミュニケーションコース
My Room 私の部屋

Phrase 表現	Alternative 他の言い方	Meaning 意味
in the middle		間中にあります
at the top	on (the) top	上にあります
at the bottom	on the bottom	下にあります
between (A) and (B)		AとBの間にあります
above ...	on top of ...	...の上にあります
below ...	under ...	...の下にあります。
on the right side		右側にあります
on the left side		左側にあります
to the left of ...		...の左側にあります
to the right of ...		...の右側にあります
in front of ...		...の前にあります
behind ...		...の後ろにあります
in the top right-hand corner		右上にあります
in the top left-hand corner		左上にあります
in the bottom right-hand corner		右下にあります
in the bottom left-hand corner		左下にあります

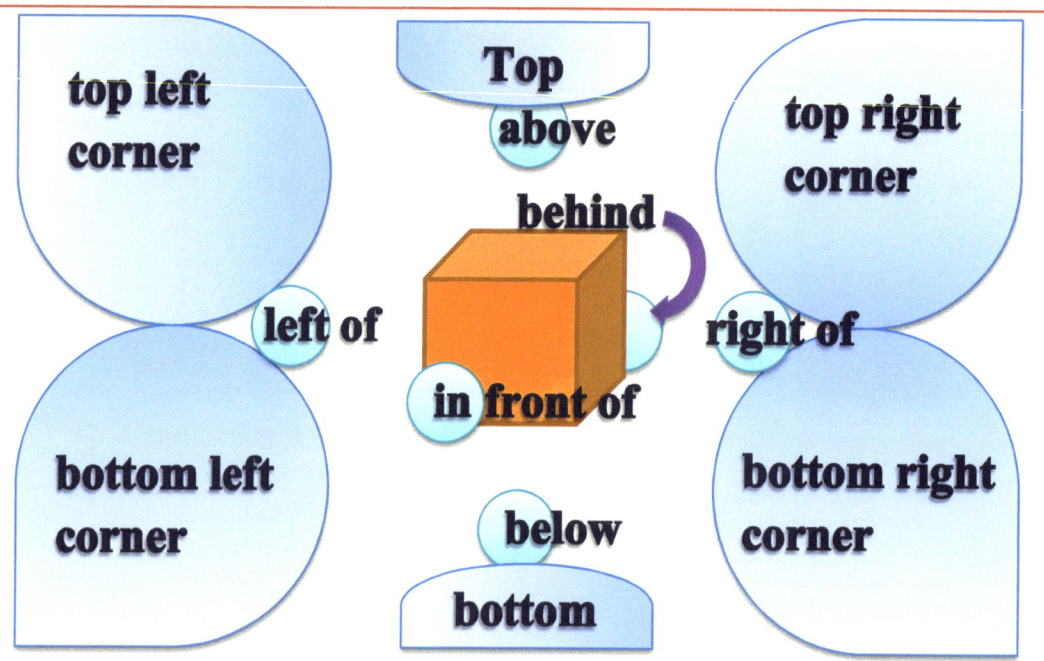

One with English コミュニケーションコース　Stage 3

My Room 私の部屋

Listening Practice:　聞く練習しましょう。

Listening Practice:　聞く練習しましょう。

Listen and place the letters. A, B, C, D, E, F, G, H, and X

Stage 3

One with English コミュニケーションコース

My Room 私の部屋

Place the letters. A, B, C, D, E, F, G, H, and X

Listen to your partner and place. A, B, C, D, E, F, G, H, and X

My Room 私の部屋

Put it into practice

B. 下線のところに適当な言葉を書きましょう。

1. E = Eric Hawkinson, J = Jun

    J: Where _____ my CDs?

    E: They are in _____ desk.

    J: Where _____ my ticket?

    E: It _____ on the table.

2. M = Michael Jordan, L = Larry Bird

    L: I found this. Is this _____ newspaper?

    M: No, it's _____, sorry.

    L: OK, I'll put it in the lost and _____.

3. Y = Yumi, K = Keiko, A = Akio

    Y: _____ is my phone?

    K: It's _____ the door.

    A: It's _____ the box _____ the door.

    Y: Thank you.

Put it into practice

C. 複数形で書いてください、正しい発音を○してみましょう。

#	名詞	複数形	発音
例	cup	cups	/s/ /z/ /iz/
1.	fan		/s/ /z/ /iz/
2.	age		/s/ /z/ /iz/
3.	potato		/s/ /z/ /iz/
4.	tray		/s/ /z/ /iz/
5.	roll		/s/ /z/ /iz/
6.	band		/s/ /z/ /iz/
7.	wish		/s/ /z/ /iz/
8.	fly		/s/ /z/ /iz/
9.	ski		/s/ /z/ /iz/
10.	winter		/s/ /z/ /iz/
11.	king		/s/ /z/ /iz/
12.	church		/s/ /z/ /iz/
13.	tear		/s/ /z/ /iz/
14.	glove		/s/ /z/ /iz/
15.	bat		/s/ /z/ /iz/
16.	crab		/s/ /z/ /iz/
17.	garage		/s/ /z/ /iz/
18.	card		/s/ /z/ /iz/
19.	place		/s/ /z/ /iz/
20.	book		/s/ /z/ /iz/

My Room 私の部屋

Put it to practice

A. 絵を見て下の正しい文章を○しましょう。

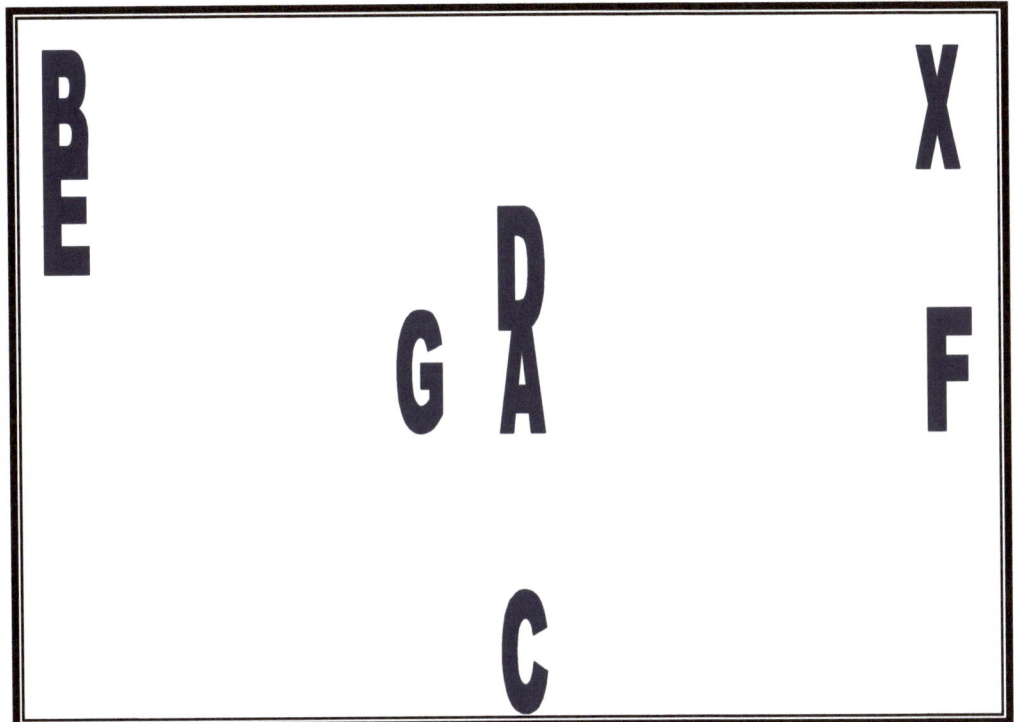

A is in the middle.
A is on the left side of G.
B is in the top right-hand corner.
X is in the top right hand corner.
F is on the left side.

C is on the bottom.
D is above A.
A is below G.
E is below B.
D is on the top.
G is on the right side of A.
C is in the middle.

Stage 3 One with English コミュニケーションコース

My Room 私の部屋

Read, read, read

Read the following descriptions of famous people. Can you guess who they are?

下に有名な人について文章が書いてあります。この人誰でしょうか？

   Our English classroom is very nice. We have a lot of space. There are 30 desks in our class. Eric has a special large desk in the front of the class. There small lockers in our class where we put our bags. It's very convenient. There is a large whiteboard in front of the desks. Next to the whiteboard there is a screen. There are many things written on the whiteboard and there is a lot of information on the screen. Eric's computer is on his desk. There are always many papers on his desk. The trash can under his desk is very small but there is a bigger one by the door under the whiteboard. We study every day in this classroom and we like it.

1. Where is the large trash can?	2. Where are the trash cans?	3. What is on Eric's desk?

Write, write, write

Think about your room. Write about what is in your room and where things are.

自分の部屋を考えましょう。ものはどこでしょうか？書きましょう。

One with English コミュニケーションコース　Stage 4

Making Friends 友達を作ろう

STAGE FOUR
Making Friends
友達を作ろう

テーマ：	Theme:
友達を作ろう 友達の紹介	Making Friends Introducing Friends
文法：	Grammar:
複数形 一般動詞 三人称 所有代名詞	Plural nouns Plain Verbs Third Person Verbs Possessive adjectives

Stage 4   One with English コミュニケーションコース
Making Friends 友達を作ろう

Dialog – "He likes salmon"

What sushi do you like?

I like shrimp. How about you?

I like shrimp too. But my brother likes salmon.

He likes salmon? Let's buy some.

Vocabulary:

単語	意味	単語	意味	単語	意味
let's	…をしよう。	sushi	寿司	how	どう
like	好き	shrimp	海老	salmon	鮭
likes	Like の三人称形	buy	買う	some	いくつの

一般動詞

	原形	三人称単数形
普通は動詞	walk	walks
	jump	jumps
子音＋y で終わる	carry	carries
	apply	applies
母音＋y で終わる	play	plays
	stay	stays
s/ch/sh/o などで終わる	watch	watches
	do	does
特別	have	has

Making Friends 友達を作ろう

Kinds of Sushi

Kinds of sushi

日本語	英語
海老	shrimp
鮪	tuna
はまち、ぶり	yellowtail
鮭	salmon
いくら	salmon roe
ほたて	scallops
いか	squid
たこ	octopus
とろ	fatty tuna
かに	crab
うなぎ	fresh water eel
あなご	sea eel
さば	blue mackerel
あわび	abalone
なまこ	sea cucumber
うに	sea urchin
青柳、蛤	clam
ひめじゃこ	giant clam
まさご	smelt roe

Stage 4 — One with English コミュニケーションコース
Making Friends 友達を作ろう

Interview and Introductions "He/She likes…"

Interview and Introductions
面接と紹介

面接	
質問	答え
1. What color do you like?	
2. What food do you eat?	
3. What sports do you play?	
4. What music do you listen to?	
5. What movie do you like?	
6. What work do you do?	
7. What car do you drive?	

三人称の文書を書きましょう	
質問	答え
1. What color do you like?	He/She like**s** _____.
2. What food do you eat?	
3. What sports do you play?	
4. What music do you listen to?	
5. What movie do you like?	
6. What work do you do?	
7. What car do you drive?	

友達を紹介しましょう。

This is my friend _____ （名前）．

He/She like**s**/eat**s** …

One with English コミュニケーションコース Stage 4

Making Friends 友達を作ろう

He/She Likes

(例)

Eric likes **science**.
エリックは理科が好きです。

Kimutaku plays **shogi**.
たくやさんはしょぎをします。

文書を書きましょう。

例: Eric likes science.
1.
2.
3.
4.
5.
6.
7.

NO WAY!　あり得ない

I believe you!　あなたを信じています。

Stage 4 — One with English コミュニケーションコース
Making Friends 友達を作ろう

Dialog – "Does he likes salmon?"

- Does your daughter like chocolate?
- Yes, she does. Why?
- I have some chocolate from America. Does she want some?
- Sure. Thank you!

Vocabulary:

単語	意味	単語	意味	単語	意味
she	彼女	from	から	have	持っている
want	欲しい	sure	もちろん	why	なぜ
do**es**	Do の三人称形	daughter	娘	some	いくつの

疑問文

文法 lesson
疑問文を作りから

Do/Doesと主語を逆にしたら疑問文になります。

彼女は…します。
She does …
Does she …?
彼女は…しますか。

One with English コミュニケーションコース Stage 4

Making Friends 友達を作ろう

Toolbox – "About our friends"

Does he like sushi?
Yes, he does.

Toolbox 1

Does he/she like ...?

彼/彼女は...が好きですか。　(教科)

science	理科	chemistry	科学
English	英語	Japanese	国語
history	歴史	geography	地理
literature	文学	P.E.	体育

Toolbox 2

Does he/she like ...?

彼/彼女は...が好きですか。　(テレビ)

comedy	喜劇	drama	ドラマ
documentary	ドキュメンタリー	suspense	サスペンス
nature	自然	talk	話し合い
news	ニュース	live music	音楽

Toolbox 3

Does he/she like ...?

彼/彼女は...が好きですか。　(趣味)

hiking	ハイキング	music	音楽
video games	テレビゲーム	movies	映画
fishing	釣り	cooking	料理
comics	まんが	art	美術

| Yes, he/she does. | はい、好きです。 | No, he/she doesn't. | いいえ、好きじゃない。 |

Stage 4 — One with English コミュニケーションコース
Making Friends 友達を作ろう

Put it to practice

箱の中に do, does, don't, doesn't を書きましょう。

1) My mother likes chocolate, but she _____ like biscuits.

2) What _____ the children wear at your school?

3) Lynn's father watches badminton on TV, but he _____ watch judo.

4) Where _____ the Masons buy their fruit?

5) _____ the cat like to sleep on the sofa?

6) Dogs love bones, but they _____ love cheese.

7) Where _____ Sam and Ben hide their CDs?

8) We eat pizza, but we _____ eat hamburgers.

9) _____ Mrs Miller read magazines?

10) _____ the boys play basketball outside?

Making Friends 友達を作ろう

Put it to practice

答えを○しましょう。

1. The dog (eat / eats) the food.

2. The cat (run / runs) in the house.

3. John (jump / jumps) on the trampoline.

4. Caleb (play / plays) with toys.

5. They (grow / grows) bigger every year.

6. My finger (hurt / hurts) because I cut it on the fence.

7. It (dig / digs) in the garden for some worms.

8. Suzy (nail / nails) the boards together to make a birdhouse.

9. Dad (shave / shaves) his whiskers each morning.

10. Mom (like / likes) to read to her kids.

11. We (sing / sings) in the shower.

12..Jenna (ride / rides) her horse around the pasture.

13. Dan (spill / spills) the milk.

Making Friends 友達を作ろう

Put it to practice

下の話は三人称で書き直しましょう。

例: **Q.** I like hiking. I go hiking on Saturdays. When I go hiking I drink tea.

A. <u>He likes hiking. He goes hiking on Saturdays. When he goes hiking he drinks tea.</u>

1. Q. I play tennis on Sunday. I don't play tennis on Saturday because I work on Saturday.

A. _____
_____
_____
_____

2. Q. I don't like sushi but I do like natto. I eat natto when I stay with my grandmother.

A. _____
_____
_____
_____

One with English コミュニケーションコース　Stage 5
MyFamily 私の家族

STAGE FIVE

My Family
私の家族

テーマ：	Theme:
家族・親戚 性格	Family/Relatives Personalities
文法：	Grammar:
所有代名詞 一番好きなもの	Possessive adjectives Favorites

Stage 5 · One with English コミュニケーションコース
My Family 私の家族

Dialog – "What's he like?"

- Have you met my brother?
- No, I haven't. What's he like?
- He's so great! He's smart and funny.
- Where does your brother live?
- He lives in Arizona with his wife.
- Really? Arizona is my favorite place!
- Let's go visit! His house is nice too.

Vocabulary:

単語	意味	単語	意味	単語	意味
my	私の	let's	…をしよう。	great	素晴らしい
your	あなたの	like	のような	smart	賢い
his	彼の	likes	Like の三人称形	funny	面白い
favorite	一番好きな	wife	奥さん	nice	よい

所有代名詞

	だれ・Who	だれの・Whose
私	me	my
彼	he	his
彼女	she	her
あなた	you	your
私たち	we	our
あなたたち	you	your
彼たち	they	their
これ・それ・あれ	it	it's
エリック	Eric	Eric's

One with English コミュニケーションコース Stage 5

MyFamily 私の家族

Family and Relatives

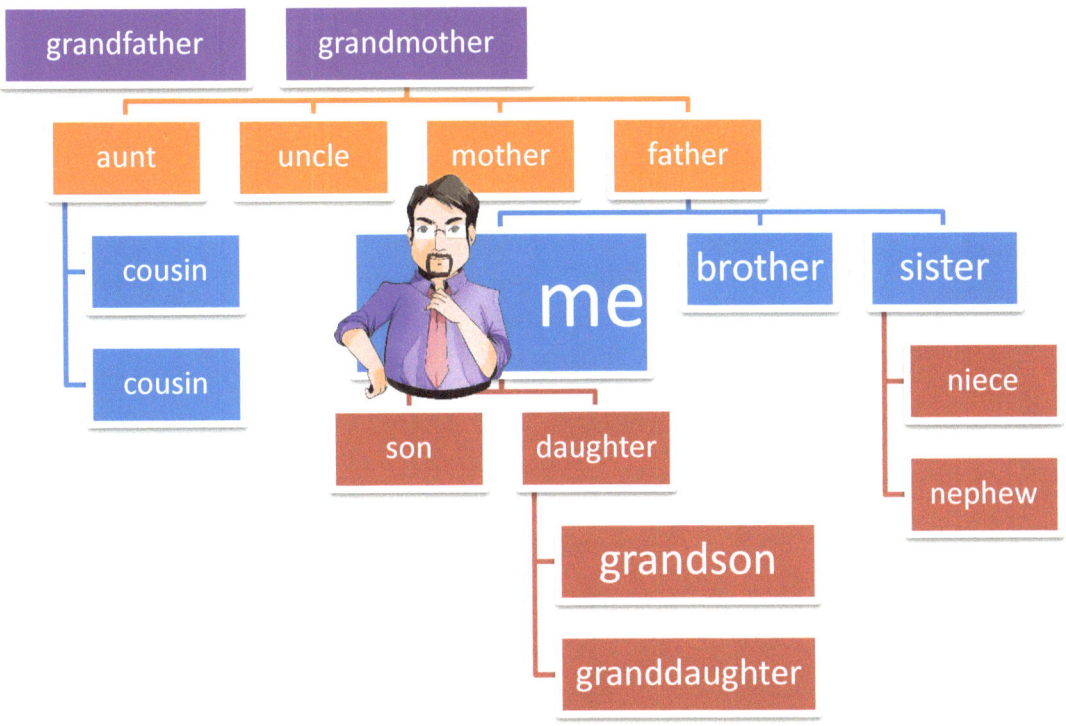

Boys 男				Girls 女			
Japanese	English	Japanese	English	Japanese	English	Japanese	English
		大祖父	great-grandfather	大祖母	great-grandmother		
夫	husband	祖父	grandfather	祖母	grandmother	妻	wife
叔父	uncle	父	father	母	mother	叔母	aunt
兄/弟	brother	息子	son	娘	daughter	姉/妹	sister
甥	nephew					姪	niece

General Family Words:

family 家族 *kazoku*	relatives 親戚 *shinseki*	siblings 兄弟 *kyoudai*	cousins いとこ *itoko*
parents 両親 *ryoushin*	children 子供 *kodomo*	~in-law 義理の~ *giri no~*	grandchild 孫 *mago*
ancestor 先祖 *senzo*	descendant 子孫 *shison*	married 結婚 *kekkon*	single 独身 *dokushin*

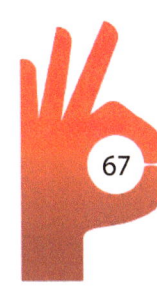

Stage 5 One with English コミュニケーションコース
My Family 私の家族

Dialog – "What is your family like?"

How many members are in your family?
Five. My mother, father and two sisters.
What is your mother like?
She is quiet and kind.
What are your sisters like?
One of them is quiet and shy and one of them is talkative and outgoing. They both are very active.

Vocabulary:

単語	意味	単語	意味	単語	意味
family	家族	mother	母	quiet	おとなしい
like	のような	father	父	kind	優しい
members	メンバー	sister	姉・妹	shy	恥ずかしい
active	活動的な	talkative	話好きな	outgoing	社交的な

Personalities 性格

		反対		
恥ずかしい	shy	⟷	社交的な	outgoing
おとなしい	quiet	⟷	話好きな	talkative
好意的な	friendly	⟷	卑劣な	mean
優しい	nice	⟷	卑劣な	mean
楽しい	fun	⟷	退屈な	boring
面白い	interesting	⟷	退屈な	boring
怠惰な	lazy	⟷	活動的な	active
賢い	smart	⟷	頭が悪い	dumb
緩やか	lenient	⟷	厳しい	strict
合理的	rational	⟷	バカ	crazy

MyFamily 私の家族

Stage 5

Interview and Introductions

Interview and Introductions
面接と紹介
"What's your family like?"

面接	
質問	答え
1. How many members in your family?	
2. What is your _____ like?	
3. What is your _____ like?	
4. What is your _____ like?	
5. What is your _____ like?	
6. What is your _____ like?	
7. What is your _____ like?	

パートナの家族について文章を書きましょう。	
質問	答え
8. How many members in your family?	He/She has ___ members in his/her family.
9. What is your _____ like?	
10. What is your _____ like?	
11. What is your _____ like?	
12. What is your _____ like?	
13. What is your _____ like?	
14. What is your _____ like?	

友達を紹介しましょう。

This is my friend _____ （名前）.

He/She has ___ members ...

His/Her mother/father is _____.

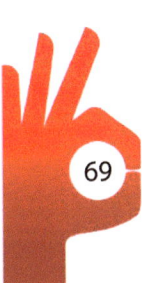

Stage 5 — My Family 私の家族

One with English コミュニケーションコース

Put it to practice

下線に my, your, his, her, our, their を書きましょう。

1. My name is Tommy. _____ mom is Helen and _____ dad is Bob. I'm _____ son.

2. My name is Lisa. _____ parents are Mary and Dave. I'm _____ daughter.

3. My name is Kevin. I have a new sister. _____ name is Betsy. My mom is Sara and my dad is Bob. _____ last name is Smith -- Sara Smith, Bob Smith, Betsy Smith, and Kevin Smith.

4. My mom is a kind person. _____ name is Kim. _____ mom is next to her. She is _____ grandma. She has white hair.

5. This is my friend Tommy and _____ grandpa.

6. This is my friend Susie and _____ grandpa.

7. This is my friend Johnny and _____ grandparents. _____ grandma is wears glasses. _____ grandpa is doesn't wear glasses.

8. Do you have a picture of you and _____ family?

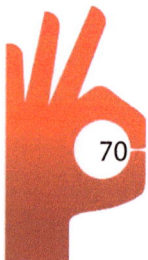

MyFamily 私の家族

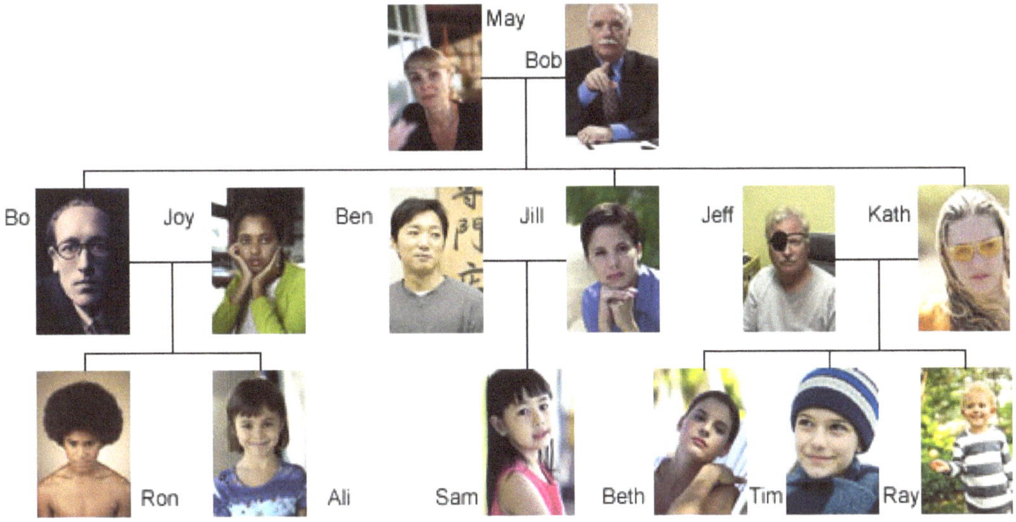

Stage 5

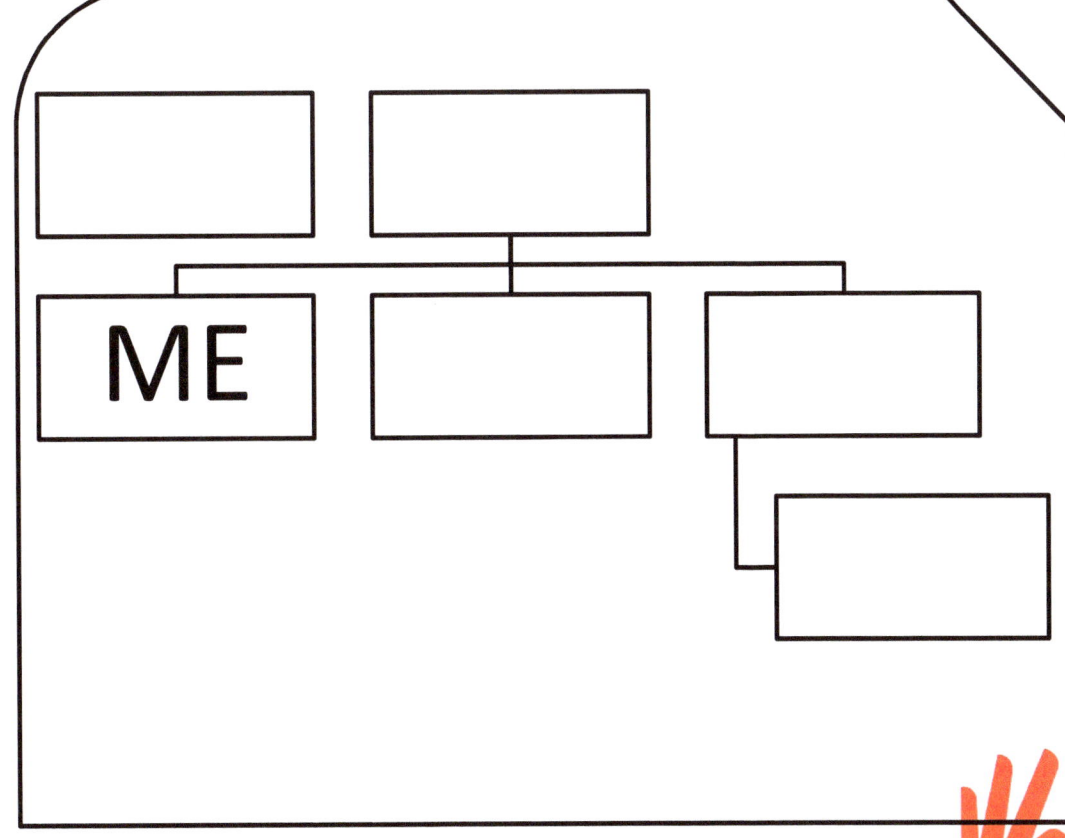

May is Tim's	Ray is Ali's
Ron is Kath's	Tim is Bob's
Ben is Beth's	May is Joy's
Beth is Bo's	Ron is Ali's
Joy is Sam's	Jill is May's

My Family Tree

ME

Stage 5 One with English コミュニケーションコース

My Family 私の家族

Read, read, read

Read the following descriptions of famous people. Can you guess who they are?

下に有名な人について文章が書いてあります。この人誰でしょうか？

> I have a very big family. I have 8 members in my immediate family. My mom and dad are kind and caring. My dad is sometimes strict. I also have 2 older sisters. They are both very active. Lisa plays tennis and Cindy is on the track team. She also is very smart! I also have 2 younger brothers. Their names are Tim and Leo. They are both quiet and shy. Tim is very lazy and doesn't help around the house. Oh! I almost forgot. The last member of my family is Annie, she is my sister's dog. Annie is smart, kind, and loyal. It's hard being is a big family but I like it. What is your family like?

1. Who is smart in the family?	2. How many girls are there in the family?	3. What is the dog like?

Write, write, write

Write about your family and their personalities.
自分の家族について書きましょう。

One with English コミュニケーションコース　Stage 6

My Schedule 私のスケジュール

STAGE SIX

My Schedule
私のスケジュール

テーマ：	Theme:
スケジュール ひまの時間	Schedules Free-time
文法：	Grammar:
どのぐらい。。。？ 程度副詞 大好き〜大嫌い	How often? Adverbs of frequency Likes and dislikes

Stage 6 — One with English コミュニケーションコース
My Schedule 私のスケジュール

Dialog – "How often do you …?"

- How often do you practice judo?
- I practice everyday. Sometimes I practice in the morning and sometimes I practice in the evening.
- How often do you play basketball?
- I play once a week. Usually on Wednesday.
- I never play basketball. But let's practice judo sometime!

Vocabulary:

単語	意味	単語	意味	単語	意味
how often	どのぐらい	practice	練習	morning	朝
everyday	毎日	sometimes	時々	evening	夕方
once	一回	week	週	usually	普通に
never	全然〜しない	sometime	いつか	but	しかし

程度副詞

Group 1 いつも〜全然しない	Group 2 毎日・毎朝・毎年	Group 3 何週間何回
always	every day	once a day
usually	every morning	once a week
often	every month	twice a month
sometimes	every evening	twice a year
rarely	every time	three times a year
never	every year	10 times a week

My Schedule 私のスケジュール

How often do you .... ?

Toolbox – "How often"

Toolbox 1

How often ...?

Group 1: Always ~ Never

always	いつも	usually	普通に
often	よく	sometimes	時々
rarely	めったに〜ない	never	全然〜ない
Once in a while	たまには		

Toolbox 2

How often ... ?

Group 2: Every…

every time	毎回	every day	毎日
every month	毎月	every morning	毎朝
every evening	毎晩	every Sunday	毎週の日曜日
every year	毎年	every week	毎週

Toolbox 3

How often... ?

Group 3: Once/Twice/x times a day/week

once	一回	twice	二回
three times	三回	four times	四回
a day	一日	a week	一週間
a month	一ヶ月	a year	一年間

１〜７まで一番よくすることを順番しましょう。

[　] I go to the beach once a year.
[　] My brother visits Japan two times every five years.
[　] Eric eats cereal every morning for breakfast.
[　] He sometimes plays tennis with his friends.
[　] She studies English three times a week.
[　] I never eat natto because I can't stand the smell.
[　] Eric plays golf two times a month.

My Schedule 私のスケジュール

How Often

1. activity	2. every ...
play tennis	every day
study English	every month
read comic books	every week
watch T.V.	every year
3. times	**4. times a ...**
once	day
twice	week
1000 times	month
10,000,000 times	year

A: Do you ①?
B: Yes, ②.
A: How often do you study?
B: I study ③ a ④?

My Schedule 私のスケジュール

Dialog – "I really like"

- I like judo but I love basketball.
- I can't stand basketball. I never play basketball but I watch basketball on T.V.
- Really? I love basketball on T.V. How often do you watch?
- I only watch it about half a dozen times a year. I like college basketball but I don't like professional basketball.
- I only watch judo once every four years.

Vocabulary:

単語	意味	単語	意味	単語	意味
love	大好き	half	半部	basketball	バスケ
like	好き	dozen	１２個	professional	プロ
don't like	好きじゃない	college	大学	judo	柔道
only	だけ	every	毎	can't stand	嫌い

大好き～大嫌い
How much do you like … ?

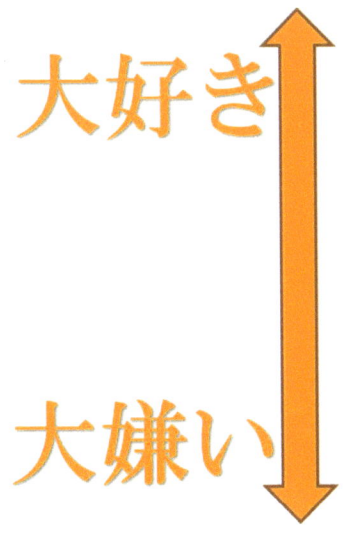

I love
I really like
I like
I don't like
I can't stand
I hate

My Schedule 私のスケジュール

Put it to practice

（　）の内の単語を使って文を書きましょう。

例：　　Q. I don't eat fish. (often)

A. I don't eat fish often. / I don't often eat fish.

1. My brother call me. (never)

2. Susan is polite. (always)

3. I go to bed before midnight. (rarely)

4. Dian doesn't work on Saturday. (usually)

5. My mother doesn't play video games. (every day)

6. Eric plays golf. （一週間二回）

7. I visit my grandparents in Kyoto. （一年間三回）

8. Do you go to the beach? （時々）

9. I listen to rock music. （めったにない）

10. How often do you study? I study. （毎日）

My Schedule 私のスケジュール

Read, read, read

	Sunday	Monday	Tuesday	Wednesday	Thursday	Friday	Saturday
7:00		Wake up	Wake up	Wake up	Wake up	Wake up	
8:00		Go to school 8:45 AM	Go to school 8:45 AM	Go to school 8:45 AM	Go to school 8:45 AM	Go to school 8:45 AM	
9:00		English Class 9:15 AM		English Class 9:15 AM		English Class 9:15 AM	Wake up 9:45 AM
10:00	Wake up						
11:00	Play basketball	Play basketball	Play basketball	Play basketball	Play basketball	Play basketball	Play basketball
Noon	Lunch with friends		Lunch with friends		Lunch with friends		Lunch with friends
1:00		Exercise	Math Class 1:30 PM	Exercise	Math Class 1:30 PM	Exercise	
3:00	Play video games			Computer Class 2:45 PM			Play video games
5:00		Study	Study	Study	Study	Study	
7:00							Dinner with my parents
8:00		Meet my Friend Eat Sushi	Watch TV		Go to the movies		Go out with friends

Read Eric's schedule and answer the following questions.
エリックのスケジュールについて下の質問を答えましょう。

1. When does Eric watch TV?

2. How much does Eric like basketball?

3. How often does Eric have English class?

4. How often does Eric play video games?

5. What time does Eric wake up?

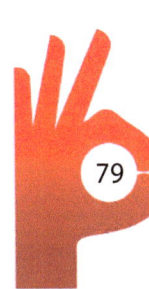

Stage 6 — One with English コミュニケーションコース
My Schedule 私のスケジュール

Write, write, write

Write about your schedule.
自分のスケジュールについて書きましょう。

	Sunday	Monday	Tuesday	Wednesday	Thursday	Friday	Saturday
Morning							
Afternoon							
Evening							

How often do you …. ?

I (一般動詞) every (day/week/Sunday/morning/など).

例： I go swimming every Sunday afternoon with my friends.

I (always/often/sometimes/hardly ever/never) (一般動詞).

例： I never go to Sushi Ro because I think Kura Zushi is better.

I (一般動詞) (once/twice/three times) a (day/week/year).

例： I play video games with my brother on the internet twice a week in the evenings.

Tell me about your week. あなたの普通の週について書きなさい。

One with English コミュニケーションコース　Stage 7
My Day Off 私の休日

STAGE SEVEN

My Day Off
私の休日

テーマ：	Theme:
活動 家事	activities chores
文法：	**Grammar:**
〜したい 〜すること好き (不定詞)	want to like to

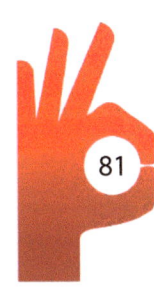

My Day Off 私の休日

Stage 7 — One with English コミュニケーションコース

Dialog – "I like to sleep in."

A: What are you doing tomorrow Cindy?

B: It's my day off so I want to sleep in. I like to sleep in on the weekends. I don't like to wake up early.

A: I like to get up early. I like to exercise in the morning. But I often want to take a nap in the afternoon.

B: I like to take naps too! I guess I like to sleep too much.

Vocabulary:

単語	意味	単語	意味	単語	意味
want	欲しい	day off	休日	nap	昼寝
want to ~	～したい	sleep in	遅く寝る	early	早い
like	好き	get up	起きる	guess	推測する
like to	していました（複数形）	wake up	起きる	~too much	～すぎる

Want to / Like to

英語	意味	例
want to~	～したい	I want to play tennis.
like to~	～すること好き	He likes to eat sushi.
don't want to~	～したくない	We don't want to go home yet.
don't like to~	～すること好きじゃない	My cat doesn't like to take a bath.

My Day Off 私の休日

Stage 7

Toolbox – "My day off"

今週末に何をしたいですか？

Toolbox 1

What do you want to do this weekend?

go to (場所)	（場所）に行きたい	visit (人)	（人）を訪問する
do laundry	洗濯する	clean my room	部屋を掃除する
run errands	用事する	practice (スポーツ)	（スポーツ）の練習する
sleep in	遅く寝る	wake up early	早く起きる
do chores	家事をする	watch TV	テレビを見る
study (教科)	（教科）を勉強する	play video games	テレビゲームをする

Q. *What do you want to do this weekend?*

A. I (want to) / (don't want to) _____.

休日になんのすること好きですか？

Toolbox 2

What do you like to do on your day off?

go to (場所)	（場所）に行きたい	visit (人)	（人）を訪問する
do laundry	洗濯する	clean my room	部屋を掃除する
run errands	用事する	practice (スポーツ)	（スポーツ）の練習する
sleep in	遅く寝る	wake up early	早く起きる
do chores	家事をする	watch TV	テレビを見る
study (教科)	（教科）を勉強する	play video games	テレビゲームをする

Q. *What do you like to do on your day off?*

A. I (like to) / (don't like to) _____.

Stage 7 One with English コミュニケーションコース
My Day Off 私の休日

Household chores

How many do you know?

a) clean off the table
b) clean up the room
c) do the laundry
d) dust the furniture
e) feed the pet(s)
f) fix up the apartment
g) hang the clothes out to dry

h) make the bed
i) mop the floor
j) mow the lawn
k) pick up the clothes
l) polish the furniture
m) put away the books
n) set the table
o) sweep the floor

p) take out the trash
q) throw out the garbage
r) tidy up the closet
s) turn off the light
t) vacuum the floor
u) wash the clothes
v) wipe down the walls
w) watch the kids

Circle the most appropriate answer.

1. Dinner is ready, please (a / b / c) and (n / o / p).
2. The dog looks hungry, please (d / e / f).
3. The grass in the front yard is too tall. Please (h / I / j).
4. I like to (s / t / u) in my room before I go to sleep.
5. Take the dirty clothes to the laundromat and (a / b / c).

6. What chores do you like to do?
7. What chores don't you like to do?

8. Can you think of any other chores you have to do?

My Day Off 私の休日

Dialog – "Household chores"

> Today is our day off and we want to catch up on household chores.

> Right! What chores do you want to do?

> I need to clean out the closet. There is a lot of garbage in the closet. After I collect it all I want to take out all the garbage in the house. How about you? What do you want to do?

> First, I hope to tidy up my desk. I study too much and there are a lot of papers. I want to put those papers in folders and save them. I don't want to put away my books though. I want to read them later.

「~すること」（不定詞）

　この用法では不定詞が動詞の目的語になる場合と主語になる場合がある。

【動詞の目的語】

I like to listen to music. 私は音楽を聴くことがすき。

Eric wants to learn Japanese history. エリックは日本の歴史を学びたい。

Yumi tried to write haiku. ユミは俳句を書こうとした。

この用法でよく使われる形

like to 動詞の原形 ~することがすき

want to 動詞の原形 ~したい

start to 動詞の原形 ~し始める

begin to 動詞の原形 ~し始める

try to 動詞の原形 ~しようとする

hope to 動詞の原形 ~することをのぞむ

※「~すること」と訳さないものもあるので注意

Stage 7 One with English コミュニケーションコース
My Day Off 私の休日

Interviews 面接
"Your day off"

面接 自分で文章で答えましょう。	
質問	答え
1. What do you want to do on your next day off?	
2. What chores do you need to do at your home soon?	
3. What do you like to on your day off?	

相手の答えを書きましょう。	
質問	答え
4. What do you want to do on your next day off?	
5. What chores do you need to do at your home soon?	
6. What do you like to on your day off?	

友達の答えで紹介しましょう。

This is my friend _____ （名前）.

He/She wants to _____.

He/She needs to _____ at his/her home.

He/She likes to _____ on his/her day off.

My Day Off 私の休日

Stage 7

One with English コミュニケーションコース

下の箱内の動詞または自由な動詞を
不定詞の形にしてみよう。

> watch, talk to, go, pay, wash, clean, listen to, play, walk, call, get, date, kiss, want, like, eat

例：I want **to watch** baseball on TV tonight.

1. Do you want _____ soccer with us outside?
2. I need _____ my room before my girlfriend comes.
3. I don't want _____ a movie star.
4. It's a nice day. I want _____ with my friends at the park.
5. We don't have school tomorrow. You don't need _____ tonight. Let's go out!
6. Where do you like _____ at the restaurant next to the station?
7. When does Yumi like _____? I think after dinner.
8. Who do you want _____, a movie star or a professional athlete?
9. Does Eric like _____. Yes, he does.
10. Does Eric want _____. No, he doesn't.

Stage 7 — One with English コミュニケーションコース

My Day Off 私の休日

Read, read, read

Read the following and answer the questions.
下の書いてあることを読んで質問を答えましょう。

> I don't have many days off but next Sunday I'm free. I want to relax but I need to catch up on some reading for my big project. I need to read three or four books and a lot of papers. I like to listen to classical music when I read, so I want to buy some new music before Sunday. My friend Yumi has a large collection of music at her house. Maybe I need to visit her soon and ask to borrow something. I guess I can relax and catch up on my work at the same time. That doesn't sound bad at all!

1. When is Eric's next day off?	2. Why does Eric need to go to Yumi's house?	3. What do you like to do when you read?

Write, write, write

Write about your day off.
あなたの休日について書きましょう。

Want to / need to / like to を使ってみましょう。

_____
_____
_____
_____
_____

One with English コミュニケーションコース　Stage 8
My Neighborhood 私の近所

STAGE EIGHT

My Neighborhood
私の近所

テーマ：	Theme:
近所 時間	Neighborhood Time
文法：	**Grammar:**
いる・ある 賛成・反対	There is/are Agree/Disagree

Stage 8 One with English コミュニケーションコース

My Neighborhood 私の近所

Dialog – "What's your neighborhood like?"

A: Excuse me. I'm your new neighbor. Is there a convenience store in the neighborhood?

B: Yes, there are two convenience stores. There is also a big supermarket.

A: Great! Please tell me more. What's the neighborhood like?

B: It's a busy and crowded neighborhood. There's a quiet park. There are a lot of stores and restaurants. But there's no hotel or movie theater.

Vocabulary:

単語	意味	単語	意味	単語	意味
There is (There's)	〜がある 単数形	big	大きい	convenience store	コンビニ
There are	〜がある 複数形	busy	忙しい	restaurant	レストラン
neighbor	となりの〜	crowded	込んでいる	hotel	面白い
neighborhood	近所	quiet	静か	movie theater	よい

〜がある (There is/There are)

Singular 単数形

There is / There's	a	big	park
	an	old	post office
	no		mall

Plural 複数形

There are	a couple of	expensive	stores
	some	nice	hotels
	a lot of	cheap	restaurants
	no		clubs

My Neighborhood 私の近所

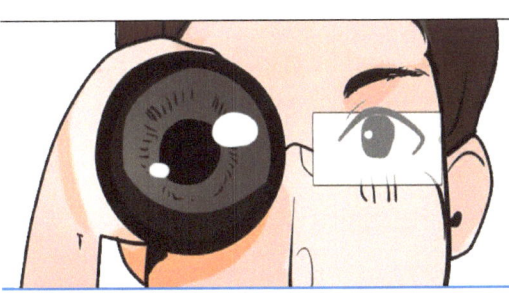

Toolbox – "In my neighborhood"

Toolbox 1

Is there a ...?

あなたの近所には...がありますか。（単数形）

station	駅	restaurant	レストラン
supermarket	スーパー	bank	銀行
museum	博物館	library	図書館
hotel	ホテル	laundromat	洗濯屋

Toolbox 2

Are there any ...?

あなたの近所には...がありますか。（複数形）

cafes	喫茶店	gas stations	ガソリンスタンド
gym	ジム	post offices	郵便局
drug stores	薬局	book stores	本屋
convenience stores	コンビニ	department stores	デパート

Toolbox 3

What's your neighborhood like?

あなたの近所はどんな近所ですか？

quiet	静か	noisy	煩い
clean	きれい	dirty	汚れている
crowded	込んでいる	spacious	広い
rural	農村	inner-city	市内

Yes, there is.
Yes, there are
(some/a few/ a lot).

はい、あります。

No, there isn't.
No, there aren't.

いいえ、ないです。

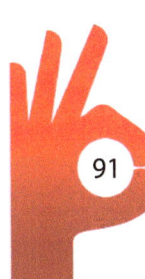

Stage 8 — One with English コミュニケーションコース
My Neighborhood 私の近所

Dialog – "Let's eat in my neighborhood"

Are you hungry?

Yes, let's eat in my neighborhood. There are a lot of good restaurants.

Is there a cheap Italian place?

Yes, there are a couple of Italian restaurants. I like Antonio's. It opens at 11 o'clock.

Great! Let's meet at 11:15. I'm hungry too!

be動詞の文なので疑問文を作る場合には be動詞を文頭にだします。
　（例）　There is a tall tree near the station.
　　→　Is there a tall tree near the station? Yes, there is. / No, there aren't.
答えるときは there をつかう。

例文
Is there a computer on the desk?　　　　机の上にコンピュータがありますか。
　　　　Yes, there is.　　　　　　　　　　はい、あります。
Are there any children in the room?　　　部屋に子どもたちはいますか。
No, there aren't.　　　　　　　　　　　　いいえ、いません。
What is there under the table?　　　　　テーブルの下には何がいますか。
　There is a cat.　　　　　　　　　　　　ネコがいます。

My Neighborhood 私の近所

Interview and Introductions
面接と紹介
"Your neighborhood"

面接 自分で文章で答えましょう。	
質問	答え
1. Is there a (銀行)?	
2. Is there a big (映画館)?	
3. Is there quiet (公園)?	
4. Are there some good (店)?	
5. Are there any (スーパー)?	
6. Are there a lot of (レストラン)?	
7. Are there any cheap (ホテル)?	

相手の答えを書きましょう。	
質問	答え
1. Is there a (銀行)?	
2. Is there a big (映画館)?	
3. Is there quiet (公園)?	
4. Are there some good (店)?	
5. Are there any (スーパー)?	
6. Are there a lot of (レストラン)?	
7. Are there any cheap (ホテル)?	

友達の近所を紹介しましょう。

This is my friend _____ （名前）．

There is / There are _____ in his/her neighborhood.

Stage 8 — My Neighborhood 私の近所

Put it to practice

下線に

There's, is, There are, are, Are there, Is there
を書きましょう。

1. _____ two.

2. There _____ a lot of people coming.

3. _____ a lot of water on the carpet.

4. There _____ a lot of noise coming from next door.

5. _____ a lot of traffic in the rush hour?

6. There _____ only one possible answer.

7. There _____ two possible answers.

8. _____ never enough time to finish it.

9. There _____ some people to see you.

10. _____ anybody there?

11. There _____ little information available.

12. _____ little time left.

13. There _____ no time like the present.

14. _____ some rice left?

15. There _____ much to say on the subject.

One with English コミュニケーションコース Stage 8

My Neighborhood 私の近所

Skills: Reading a Map

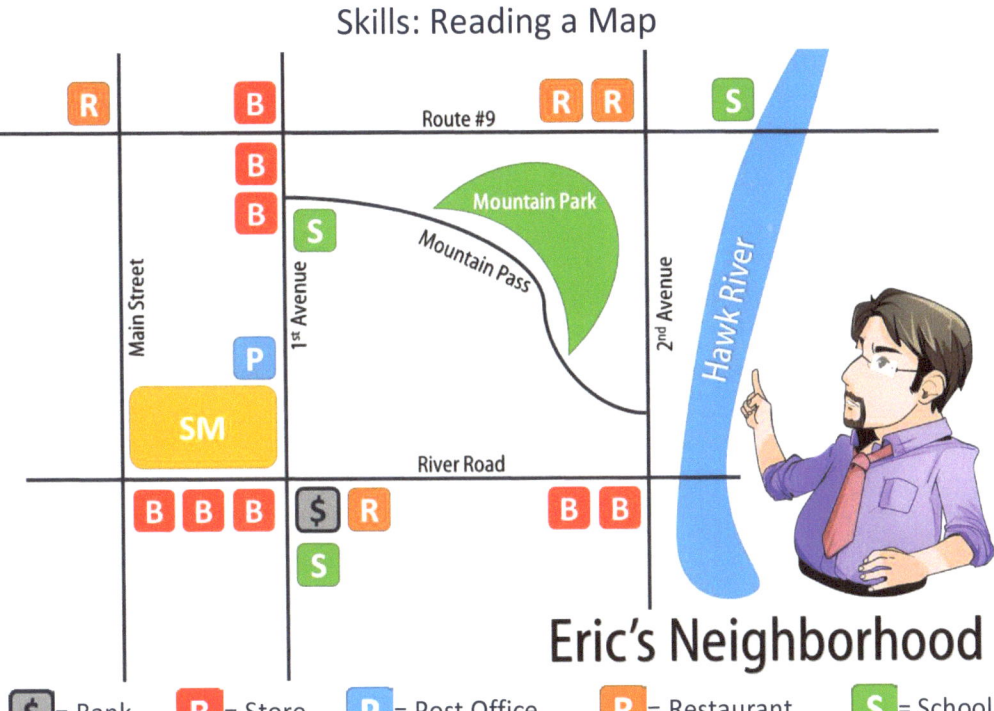

$ = Bank   B = Store   P = Post Office   R = Restaurant   S = School

上の地図をみて下の問題を答えましょう。

True of False

1. There is a post office in Eric's Neighborhood.	T / F
2. There is a bank on Main Street.	T / F
3. There are a lot of stores on River Road.	T / F
4. There are no schools on 1st Avenue.	T / F
5. There is a big park and called Mountain Pass.	T / F

6. How many schools are there?

7. Where is the post office?

8. Is there a school on Mountain Pass?

9. What is in Eric's Neighborhood?

Stage 8 — One with English コミュニケーションコース

My Neighborhood 私の近所

Read, read, read

Read the following description of the neighborhood. Can you guess who they are?

下に近所について文章が書いてあります。どんな近所でしょうか？

> Cindy and Jun come from very different neighborhoods. Cindy comes from the inner-city. It's a crowded, dirty, and very busy place. There are many expensive restaurants and even a large sports stadium in her neighborhood. There are no big parks. Jun's neighborhood is in a rural area. There isn't any movie theatres or department stores. There are a few farms, some big mountains, and a wonderful ski resort. He likes to ski every winter there.

1. Are there restaurants in Cindy's neighborhood?	2. What is in Jun's neighborhood?	3. Do you want to live in Jun's or Cindy's neighborhood? Why?

Write, write, write

What is your neighborhood like?
あなたの近所はどんな近所ですか？

One with English コミュニケーションコース　Stage 9

My Driver's Test 私の運転免許試験

STAGE NINE

My Driver's Test
私の運転免許試験

テーマ：	Theme:
運転 ルール	driving rules
文法：	Grammar:
不定詞	have to don't have to need to must/mustn't

Stage 9 — One with English コミュニケーションコース
My Driver's Test 私の運転免許試験

Dialog – "My driver's test"

A: I am trying to get my driver's license. There are many things I have to know.

B: There are many rules you need to know. For example, we drive on the left side in America and we drive on the left side in Japan.

A: In Japan, we mustn't turn left while the traffic light is red. In America, you don't have to wait for a green light to turn right.

B: There are many rules you must obey to be a safe driver. You need to practice and get experience. Remember, safety first!

Vocabulary:

単語	意味	単語	意味	単語	意味
have to ~	～しなければならない	drive	運転する	rule	法則 ルール
need to ~	～すろことが必要	driver	運転手	traffic light	信号機
don't have to ~	～しなくてもいい	right	右	example	例
must	～しなければならない	left	左	practice	練習する
mustn't	～ならない	turn	曲がる	experience	経験

have to/need to/must

言葉	意味	例
have to	～しなければならない	I have to go home.
don't have to	～しなけくてもいい	We don't have to go to school today.
need to	～することが必要	She needs to sleep.
don't need to	～しなけくてもいい	They don't need to take a break.
must	～しなければならない	We all must breathe.
must not (mustn't)	～てならない	You mustn't use your phone on the train.

My Driver's Test 私の運転免許試験

Toolbox – "Do you have to _____ today?"

Toolbox 1

Do you have to _____ today?

あなた今日は（_____）をしなければならないですか？

practice	練習する	study	勉強する
take a test	試験をとる	write a report	レポートを書く
go to class	授業にいく	prepare for the test	試験のために準備する
visit the teacher	先生に訪問する	work	働く

Q. Do you have to _____ today?

A. Yes, I do. / No, I don't

Toolbox 3

What do you need to do tomorrow?

明日はなにをしなければならないですか？

practice	練習する	study	勉強する
take a test	試験をとる	write a report	レポートを書く
go to class	授業にいく	prepare for the test	試験のために準備する
visit the teacher	先生に訪問する	work	働く

Q. What do you need to do tomorrow?

A.

I have to _____.

I don't have to _____.

I need to _____.

I don't need to _____.

I must _____.

I mustn't _____.

Stage 9 — One with English コミュニケーションコース

My Driver's Test 私の運転免許試験

Do you know these American road signs?
Use (have to/don't have to/must/mustn't/need to/don't need to) to explain the rule.
このアメリカのサインの意味が知っていますか？
（have to/don't have to/must/mustn't/need to/don't need to）
を使ってサインの意味を推測して文章を書きましょう。

SIGN	RULE
	You must stop here. You need to stop.

My Driver's Test 私の運転免許試験

Dialog – "The creepy old house"

How old do you have to be to get a driver's license in America?

You must be sixteen years old to get a driver's license?

What do you have to do to get a driver's license in America?

The rules are different in every state in America. In Arizona we have to take a test and pay a fee. In Arizona we don't have to renew our license until we turn sixty years old.

意味

must と have to は、両方とも中学校で学習します。なぜか印象に残る単語なので、英語が苦手な方でも覚えている、何かと魅力的な言葉です。

そのお陰もあって、意味が「〜しなければならない」というのは、すでに皆さんご存知だと思います。さらに「must ＝ have to」であることも有名です。

しかし実際は、must と have to は少し意味が異なります。その違いは以下の通りです。

「〜しなければならない」の基本的な意味は have to と同じですが、must は「主観的に〜しなければならない」と思う場合に使います。

"主観的"ではピンとこないかもしれませんが、簡単には「個人的にそう思う場合」に使うのが must です。

また、must には「命令」の意味が含まれるので、使う場合には注意が必要です。

「〜しなければならない」の基本的な意味は must と同じですが、have to は「客観的に〜しなければならない」場合に使います。

"客観的"ではピンとこないかもしれませんが、簡単には「誰もがそう思う場合」に使うのが have to です。

違いがよくわかるように、must の例文 1 を have to で表します。

My Driver's Test 私の運転免許試験

Interview and Introductions
面接と紹介
"Driving Rules"

面接 自分で文章で答えましょう。	
質問	答え
1. What is one important rule for driving in your country?	
2. What is one rule you don't need for driving in your country?	
3. What is a new rule you need for driving in your country?	

相手の答えを書きましょう。	
質問	答え
4. What is one important rule for driving in your country?	
5. What is one rule you don't need for driving in your country?	
6. What is a new rule you need for driving in your country?	

友達の趣味を紹介しましょう。

This is my friend _____ （名前）.

He/She thinks _____ is an important rule.

He/She thinks _____ is a rule we don't need.

My friend made a new rule for driving and it is

_____.

My Driver's Test 私の運転免許試験

have to または don't have to に次の動詞の１つを選んで、文を完成しましょう。

study   wear   practice   go   speak

1. Baseball players on our team _____ five times a week.

2. Students in Japan _____ a uniform in high school.

3. We have a test next week so we _____.

4. Today is a holiday. I _____ to school.

5. You _____ English when you travel to America.

あなたや家族、友達がしなければならないこと、しなくていいことを書きましょう。

例：**(every morning)**   **I have to wake up early every morning.**

1. (every day)
   _____

2. (tomorrow)
   _____

3. (next week)
   _____

4. (every Saturday)
   _____

Stage 9 — My Driver's Test 私の運転免許試験

One with English コミュニケーションコース

Read, read, read

Read the following and answer the questions.
下の書いてあることを読んで質問を答えましょう。

Eric's son is 15 years old. He has to prepare to get his driver's license when we turns 16 years old. He lives in Arizona and you have to pass a written test and a driving test to get a license. The written test has 25 questions about the rules of driving. You have to know all of them to pass the test. You also have to take a driving test. You must follow all the rules of driving and drive very safely to pass the test. You also have to take an eye exam. The good thing about getting a driver's license in Arizona is that you don't have to renew your license until you turn 60 years old. So Eric's son doesn't have to renew his license for a very long time.

1. How old do you have to be in Arizona to get your driver's license?	2. What do you have to do to get your driver's license in Arizona?	3. What do you have to do in your country to get a driver's license?

Write, write, write

Write about the rules of your favorite sport.
あなたの好きな巣スポーツのルールについて書きましょう。？

One with English コミュニケーションコース Stage 10

My Hobbies 私の趣味

STAGE TEN

My Hobbies
私の趣味

テーマ：	Theme:
スポーツ	Sports
趣味	Hobbies
天気	Weather
文法：	Grammar:
現在進行形	Present Continuous is/am/are + ~ing

Stage 10 — One with English コミュニケーションコース

My Hobbies 私の趣味

Dialog – "What are you doing?"

A: What are you doing Mr. Hawkinson? Are you playing basketball?

B: Yes, I am. I am shooting free-throws. I am practicing for a game next week.

A: Keep it up! I'm just taking a break. I'm practicing judo today.

B: That's nice. I like watching judo on TV. Do you like watching basketball? Please come see our game this weekend.

Vocabulary:

単語	意味	単語	意味	単語	意味
playing	play の現在進行形	join	入る	doing	している
practicing	practice の現在進行形	break	休憩	free-throw	フリースロー
watching	watch の現在進行形	game	ゲーム	basketball	バスケ
shooting	shoot の現在進行形	weekend	週末	judo	柔道

動詞＋ing＝進行形

	原形	三人称単数形
たいていの動詞…そのまま ing をつける	play read	playing reading
e で終わる動詞…e をとって ing をつける	take use	taking using
＜短母音＋子音字＞で終わる動詞…子音字を重ねて ing をつける	stop drop	stopping dropping
ie で終わる動詞…ie を y に変えて ing をつける	lie die	lying dying

am/is/are （be 動詞）＋~ing ＝ 現在進行形

106

My Hobbies 私の趣味

Stage 10

[現在形] He plays baseball. 彼は野球をします。

[進行形] He is playing baseball. 彼は野球をしています。

Toolbox – "My Hobbies"

Toolbox 1 — What are you playing?

何をやっていますか？（スポーツ）

basketball	バスケ	baseball	野球
ice hockey	アイスホッケー	soccer	サッカー
football	アメリカンフットボール	badminton	バドミントン
tennis	テニス	volleyball	バレーボール

Q. What are you playing? A. I'm playing _____.

Toolbox 2 — What are you doing?

何をしていますか？（趣味）

reading books	読書	making movies	映画を作る
bowling	ボーリング	listening to music	音楽を聞く
looking at the stars	星を見ている	painting	絵画
playing the piano	ピアノを引く	fishing	釣りをする

Q. What are you doing? A. I am _____.

Toolbox 3 — Are you _____?

_____をしていますか？（現在進行形）

cooking	料理をする	dancing	踊る
blogging	ブログを書く	writing	著作
gaming	ゲームする	taking pictures	写真術
chatting	チャットする	hiking	ハイキング

Q. Are you _____? A. Yes, I am. No, I'm not.

Stage 10 — One with English コミュニケーションコース
My Hobbies 私の趣味

My hobbies.
嘘ゲーム

嘘でもよいで自分の趣味について文書を書きましょう。

例: I like playing soccer. 　　I don't like reading books.
1.
2.
3.
4.
5.
6.
7.

NO WAY!　　あり得ない

I believe you!　　あなたを信じています。

My Hobbies 私の趣味

Dialog – "What are your hobbies?"

> What are your hobbies Cindy?
>
> I like shopping. I am always online surfing the web for clothes.
>
> That sounds like an expensive hobby.
>
> It is. How about you Eric? I hear you like astronomy and photography.
>
> That's true! At night I like looking at the stars. I also like taking pictures of nature.

主語＋be 動詞＋〜ing ＋〜.
現在進行形の英作文の間違いで一番多いのは、be 動詞を忘れることです。ing 形にするのはもちろん、be 動詞も忘れずにつけて下さい。Be 動詞は主語に合わせて am, is, are のどれかを選択します。

例文：　私はテレビをみています。

⇒　まずは単語に
私は　テレビを　　みています。
(I)　　(TV)　　(am watching)

⇒　これを　主語＋be 動詞＋〜ing ＋〜．に並べると、
I am watching TV.（完成）

この単元でよく出題されるのが、進行形の文に直す問題です。現在形と進行形の例文を下に挙げますので、違いを見比べて下さい。
また、「今」という言葉がつくこともありますので、その場合は文末に now をつけて下さい。

Stage 10 One with English コミュニケーションコース

My Hobbies 私の趣味

Interview and Introductions
面接と紹介
"Our Hobbies"

面接 自分で文章で答えましょう。	
質問	答え
1. What are your hobbies?	
2. How often do you do your hobby?	
3. Are there any hobbies you would like to try?	

相手の答えを書きましょう。	
質問	答え
4. What are your hobbies?	
5. How often do you do your hobby?	
6. Are there any hobbies you would like to try?	

友達の趣味を紹介しましょう。

This is my friend _____ （名前）．

His/Her hobby is _____．

He/She is （趣味：_____） （どのぐらい）．

He/She wants to try _____．

My Hobbies 私の趣味

まず be 動詞を○して
下線に ( ) の中の動詞を ING 形書きましょう。

1. What (is / am / are) we _____ for dinner? (have)
2. I (is / am / are) _____ a book. (read)
3. The children (is / am / are) _____ dodge ball. (play)
4. When (is / am / are) you _____ home? (come)
5. The dog (is / am / are) _____ under the table. (sit)
6. (Is / Am / Are) Tim and Allen _____ again? (argue)
7. Yumi (is / am / are) _____ on the mountain. (ski)
8. My computer (is / am / are) _____ up. (boot)
9. These diamonds (is / am / are) _____ in the light. (shine)
10. Our team (is / am / are) _____ the game. (win)

次の質問に短縮形を使って自由に答えましょう。

（例：**Yes, he is / No, we aren't**）

1. Are you playing games? _____
2. Is it raining? _____
3. Are we studying English? _____
4. Am I talking too much? _____

Stage 10 — One with English コミュニケーションコース

My Hobbies 私の趣味

Read, read, read

Read the following and answer the questions.
下にエリックいついて文章が書いてあります。質問を答えましょう。

My brother and I are very close. We have the same hobbies. We are often chatting online. He uses his PC and I use my tablet. We like playing games together. We play word games and shooting games. I live in a different country than my brother. When I am sleeping, he is working. When I am finishing work, he is sleeping. So, it's hard to find time to play games online, but we do. My brother and I also like photography. We often share the photos we take. I am now saving money for a new camera.		
1. What are Eric's hobbies?	2. What is Eric doing when his brother is sleeping?	3. Are you saving money for something? What is it?

Write, write, write

What are your hobbies? What are your friends,/family members, hobbies?
あなたの趣味は何しょうか？あなたの友達や家族の趣味は？

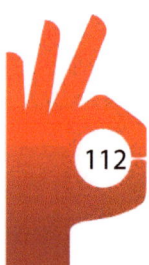

One with English コミュニケーションコース　Stage 11

My Favorite Things 私の好きなもの

STAGE ELEVEN

My Favorite Things
私の好きなもの

テーマ：	Theme:
好きなもの 値段	Favorites Prices
文法：	Grammar:
過去 BE 動詞	Past Tense Be Verbs (was, were)

Stage 11 — One with English コミュニケーションコース
My Favorite Things 私の好きなもの

Dialog – "This is my favorite thing."

A: What is that you're holding in your hand Eric?

B: This is my telescope. I am using it to look at the stars. It's my favorite thing.

A: Was it expensive? How much was it? I like looking at the stars too. I think I want one.

B: There are many different kinds of telescopes. This one was fifty thousand yen. But there were telescopes at the same store for only 5000 yen.

Vocabulary:

単語	意味	単語	意味	単語	意味
was	is, am の過去形	using	use の現在進行形	kinds	類い
were	are の過去形	holding	hold（持つ）の現在進行形	I think	〜と思う
there was	ありました（単数形）	telescope	望遠鏡	same	同じ
there were	ありました（複数形）	different	別個	only	だけ

過去形の BE 動詞

過去形Be動詞

was		were
• I • He • She	• It • This • That • 名前	• You • We • They • These • Those

My Favorite Things 私の好きなもの

Toolbox – "My Favorite Things"

Toolbox 1

What is your favorite thing?

一番好きな持っているものはなんですか？

computer	コンピューター	wallet	財布
watch	時計	sunglasses	サングラス
cell phone	携帯電話	bicycle	自転車
car	車	diary	日記

Q. What is your favorite thing? A. It's my _____.

Toolbox 2

What was your first favorite thing?

初めっての大好きなものは何でしたか？

comic book	マンガ	radio	ラジオ
game console	ゲーム機	toy	おもちゃ
doll	人形	earrings	ピアス
baseball bat	バット	necklace	ネックレス

Q. What was your first favorite thing? A. It was my _____.

Toolbox 3

How much was your _____?

あなたの_____はいくらでしたか？

bag	かばん	pen	ペン
key chain	キーホルダー	hat	帽子
textbook	教科書	case	いれもの
ring	チャットする	bracelet	ブレスレット

Q. How much was your _____? A. It was _____.

Stage 11　One with English コミュニケーションコース

My Favorite Things 私の好きなもの

My Favorite things

嘘ゲーム

嘘でもよいで自分の好きなものについて文書を書きましょう。

例: My favorite thing is my car.　　My favorite thing wasn't my blanket.
1. My favorite thing is my _____.
2. My first favorite thing was my _____.
3. My favorite thing isn't my _____
4.
5.
6.
7.

NO WAY!　　あり得ない

I believe you!　　あなたを信じています。

My Favorite Things 私の好きなもの

Dialog – "This is my favorite thing"

This is my favorite thing in the world. It's a necklace. I was my grandmother's.

It's beautiful! It looks expensive too.

I don't think was very expensive, but it is very old. It was my grandmother's and then it was my mother's. It has a couple of diamonds on it. They are so shinny.

It sounds like it is very special to you.

be 動詞過去形の使い分け

be 動詞の現在形がわからない、知らない人はまずは be 動詞の現在形から勉強して下さい。ここからは、be 動詞の現在形を理解していることを前提として解説を進めていきます。

be 動詞の過去形には二つの種類があります。

am , is の場合…was
are の場合…were
過去形はこの二つを覚えて下さい。では例文です。現在形と同じ例文を過去形にしてみます。

例文 1. :
I was a student. （私は生徒でした。）
He was a doctor. （彼は医者だった。）
She was at home. （彼女は家にいた。）
This was an apple. （これはリンゴでした。）
That was a ball. （あれはボールでした。）

例文 2. :
You were a tennis player.
　（あなたはテニスの選手でした。）
They were my friends.
　（彼らは私の友人でした。）

Stage 11 — One with English コミュニケーションコース
My Favorite Things 私の好きなもの

Interview and Introductions
面接と紹介
"Our Favorite Things"

面接 自分で文章で答えましょう。	
質問	答え
1. What is your favorite thing?	
2. How much was it?	
3. When did you get it?	

相手の答えを書きましょう。	
質問	答え
4. What is your favorite thing?	
5. How much was it?	
6. When did you get it?	

友達の趣味を紹介しましょう。

This is my friend _____（名前）.

His/Her favorite thing is her/his _____.

It was _____ yen/dollars.

My Favorite Things 私の好きなもの

現在形の am/are/is/am not/isn't/aren't　または
過去形の　was/were/wasn't/weren't　を書き入れましょう。

1. Last year she _____ 22, so she _____ 23 now.
2. The weather _____ nice today, but it _____ very cold yesterday.
3. I _____ hungry this morning. I didn't eat breakfast.
4. Where _____ you at 9 o'clock? You missed our class.
5. I like your earrings. _____ they expensive?
6. About the hotel room last week, the room _____ small, and it _____ very clean.
7. Yesterday _____ a holiday, so campus _____ closed.
8. This _____ my favorite song playing on the radio.
9. _____ Eric and Yumi at the party last night? No, they _____.
10. Where are my keys? They _____ on the table just a minute ago.
11. _____ you playing games? We need to stop and study!
12. I _____ happy with my score on the practice test. But, I _____ happy with my poor score today.

Stage 11 One with English コミュニケーションコース

My Favorite Things 私の好きなもの

Read, read, read

Read the following and answer the questions.
下にシンディーの大事なものいついて文章が書いてあります。
質問を答えましょう。

This is Cindy's favorite book. It was free. She reads it again and again. She likes the book because the story is about the future and space travel. She wants to be an astronaut. It was her dream since she was small. She dreams about going to distant worlds. It is her favorite story and she talks about it a lot with other fans of the book on a fan website. The other fans on the website were happy to share their ideas about the future with her. She visits the website very often.		
1. What is Cindy's favorite story about?	2. Who does Cindy talk about her favorite story with?	3. What is your favorite story? Why?

Write, write, write

What are your favorite things? What were your favorite things growing up?
あなたの好きなものは？こどもの時は？
いろいろなものを説明しましょう。

One with English コミュニケーションコース　Stage 12

My House Growing Up 私の育てた家

STAGE TWELEVE

My House Growing Up
私の育った家

テーマ：	Theme:
部屋	rooms
家具	furniture
文法：	**Grammar:**
There+過去 BE 動詞	There (was, were)

Stage 12 — One with English コミュニケーションコース
My House Growing Up 私の育てた家

Dialog – "My house growing up"

A: What was your home like growing up? What kinds of things were there in your house?

B: Well, I'm from Japan. There were a couple of tatami rooms. So there weren't any beds. There were futons. There was a kotasu in the living room.

A: A kotatsu? That is like a table, right?

B: Yeah. We use it in the winter. It is a table and also a heater. They are in almost every Japanese home.

Vocabulary:

単語	意味	単語	意味	単語	意味
was	is, am の過去形	wasn't	isn't, am not の過去形	living room	居間
were	are の過去形	weren't	aren't の過去形	table	テーブル
there was	ありました（単数形）	growing up	grow up 育つ	winter	冬
there were	ありました（複数形）	a couple of	二つの	heater	ヒーター

There+過去形のBE動詞

ある	ない	あった	なかった
• There's • There are	• There isn't • There aren't	• There was • There wasn't	• There wasn't • There weren't

My House Growing Up 私の育てた家

One with English コミュニケーションコース — Stage 12

Toolbox – "What was in your room this morning?"

Toolbox 1

Is there a ____ in your home?

あなたの家に_____がありますか？

living room	居間	bathroom	トイレ
bedroom	寝室	garage	車庫
kitchen	台所	den/study	書斎
entrance hall	玄関	closet	クローゼット

Q. *Is there a ____ in your home?*
A. Yes, there is. / No, there isn't.

Toolbox 2

Was there a ____ in your home growing up?

育った家に_____がありましたか？

living room	居間	bathroom	トイレ
bedroom	寝室	garage	車庫
kitchen	台所	den/study	書斎
entrance hall	玄関	closet	クローゼット

Q. *Was there a ____ in your home?*
A. Yes, there was. / No, there wasn't.

Toolbox 3

What was in your room growing up?

育った部屋に何がありましたか？

table	テーブル	lamp	ランプ
chair	椅子	couch/sofa	カウチ・ソファ
bed	ベッド	cabinet	いれもの
desk	机	bookcase	本棚

Q. *What was in your room growing up?*
A. There was a _____. / There were some _____(s).

Stage 12 — One with English コミュニケーションコース

My House Growing Up 私の育てた家

Rooms

How many do you know?

A
- anteroom
- armory
- assembly room
- attic

B
- backroom
- ballroom
- basement
- bathroom
- bedroom
- boardroom
- boiler room
- boudoir
- breakfast nook
- breakfast room

C
- cabin
- cell
- cellar
- chamber
- changing room
- chapel
- classroom
- clean room
- cloakroom
- cold room
- common room
- conference room
- conservatory
- control room
- courtroom
- cubby

D
- darkroom
- den
- dining room
- dormitory
- drawing room
- dressing room
- dungeon

E
- emergency room
- engine room
- entry

F
- family room
- fitting room
- formal dining room
- foyer
- front room

G
- game room
- garage
- garret
- great room
- green room
- grotto
- guest room
- gym

H
- hall
- hallway
- homeroom
- hospital room
- hotel room

I
- inglenook

J
- jail cell

K
- keep
- kitchen
- kitchenette

L
- ladies' room
- larder
- laundry room
- library
- living room
- lobby
- locker room
- loft
- lounge
- lunchroom

M
- maid's room
- mailroom
- men's room
- morning room
- motel room
- mud room

N
- newsroom
- nursery

O
- office
- operating room

P
- panic room
- pantry
- parlor
- playroom
- pool room
- powder room
- prison cell

R
- rec room
- recovery room
- restroom room
- rumpus room

S
- salesroom
- salon
- schoolroom
- screen porch
- scullery
- showroom
- sick room
- sitting room
- solarium
- staff room
- stateroom
- stockroom
- storeroom
- studio
- study
- suite
- sunroom

T
- tack room

U
- utility room

V
- vestibule
- visitor's room

W
- waiting room
- wardroom
- washroom
- water closet
- weight room
- wine cellar
- women's room
- workroom

My House Growing Up 私の育てた家

Dialog – "My House Growing Up"

What was your home like growing up? What kinds of things were there in your house?

Well, I'm from Japan. There were a couple of tatami rooms. So there weren't any beds. There were futons. There was a kotasu in the living room.

A kotatsu? That is like a table, right?

Yeah. We use it in the winter. It is a table and also a heater. They are in almost every Japanese home.

不特定の(まだよくわからない)ものが[ある，いる]は[There is ～，There are ～]で表す。

ものが1つのときは There is ～　　　　ものが複数(2つ以上)のときは There are
～(ある) 1冊の本が 机の上にある。　　(ある) 3冊の本が 机の上にある。

There is a book on the desk.　There are three books on the desk.

[過去形] は [There was ～]，[There were ～]

(ある) 1冊の本が 机の上にあった。 (ある) 3冊の本が 机の上にあった。

There was a book on the desk.　There were three books on the desk.

[疑問文] にするときは [be 動詞を前に置く]。答えるときも [there is (

(ある) 1冊の本が 机の上にあるか。　　(ある) 3冊の本が 机の上にあったか。

Is there a book on the desk? Were there three books on the desk?

Yes, there is. はい、あります。Yes, there were. はい、ありました。

No, there is not. いいえ、ありません。No, there weren't. いいえ、なかった。

Stage 12 One with English コミュニケーションコース

My House Growing Up 私の育てた家

Interview and Introductions
面接と紹介
"My House Growing Up"

面接 自分で文章で答えましょう。	
質問	答え
1. What is in your home?	
2. What was in your home growing up?	
3. What was in your (living room, kitchen, bedroom, entrance hall?) growing up?	

相手の答えを書きましょう。	
質問	答え
4. What is in your home?	
5. What was in your home growing up?	
6. What was in your (living room, kitchen, bedroom, entrance hall?) growing up?	

友達の趣味を紹介しましょう。

This is my friend _____ （名前）.

There (were / was) … in (his/her) home growing up.

There (was/were) … in (his/her) (部屋).

There (was/were) … in (his/her) (部屋).

There (was/were) … in (his/her) (部屋).

My House Growing Up 私の育てた家

現在形の there is / are / isn't / aren't
または
過去形の there was / were / wasn't / weren't
を書き入れましょう。

1. _____ a terrible earthquake in Japan in 2005.
2. The cake _____ on the table when I arrived home.
3. _____ many apples left when I came back home yesterday.
4. How many children _____ at the party?
5. _____ any water in the bottle? No, _____ any!
6. _____ a new student in your class last week? Yes, _____.
7. _____ any students in the library at 3 o'clock yesterday.
8. I think _____ a boy waiting for you yesterday.
9. _____ any people at the museum?
10. _____ any chicken left when I arrived home at lunchtime.
11. _____ any water in the fridge last night? I don't think so.
12. Eric is eating all the cheese! _____ only one piece left!

My House Growing Up 私の育てた家

Read, read, read

Read the following and answer the questions.
下の書いてあることを読んで質問を答えましょう。

> My house wasn't very big when I was growing up. There were three bedrooms. One bedroom was my father's den. One bedroom was for my brother and I. The other bedroom was for my parents. There were bunk beds in our room. I was on the top bunk. In the living room, there were a couple of chairs and a sofa. There was a small refrigerator and oven in the kitchen. There was a huge waterbed in my parents' bedroom. There were TVs in all of the bedrooms and the living room. There wasn't an entrance hall or a garage. My brother and I were always playing games in our room. It was a small house, but we were happy there.

1. What was in Eric's room?	2. How many TVs did Eric have in his house when he was growing up?	3. How many bedrooms were in your house when you were growing up? Did you share a room? With who?

Write, write, write

What was in your house growing up? What rooms were there?
あなたの育てた家は何がありましたか？　何の部屋？　家具は？

One with English コミュニケーションコース Stage 13
My Nightmare 私の悪夢

STAGE THIRTEEN

私の悪夢 My Nightmare

テーマ：	Theme:
夢・悪夢	dreams/nightmares
周囲	surroundings
恐怖	fears
文法：	**Grammar:**
過去進行形	(was, were) 〜 ing

Stage 13 — One with English コミュニケーションコース
My Nightmare 私の悪夢

Dialog – "My house growing up"

A: You were late to class this morning, Jun. Is everything OK?

B: I'm sorry, but I overslept. I was having terrible nightmares all night. So I couldn't sleep.

A: Oh my! What was your dream about?

B: I was in a dark and foggy field. There were scary wolves chasing me. They were running very fast. I was hiding in some thick bushes. I fear wild dogs.

Vocabulary:

単語	意味	単語	意味	単語	意味
was	is, am の過去形	bush	藪	fear	恐怖
were	are の過去形	hide	隠れる	fog	霧
was ~ing	していました（単数形）	could	can の過去形	foggy	霧深い
were ~ing	していました（複数形）	overslept	oversleep の過去形	thick	もうもう

過去形の BE 動詞 + ~ing

主語	ＢＥ動詞	進行形
I	was	reading a book.
They	were	playing cards.
We	weren't	studying English.

疑問

Were they playing soccer? Yes, they were.

Was the computer on? No, it wasn't

My Nightmare 私の悪夢

Stage 13 — One with English コミュニケーションコース

Toolbox – "What is your fear?"

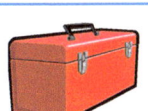

Toolbox 1

What is your fear?

あなたの恐怖はなんですか？

ghosts	おばけ	injections	注射
wolves	狼	lightning thunder	雷
heights	高いところ	flying	飛んでいる
snakes	蛇	tight spaces	狭いところ

Q. What is your fear?

A. I fear _____.

Toolbox 2

Do you think _____ places are scary?

_____の場所が怖いと思いますか？

dark	くらい	deserted	人気のない
crowded	込んでいる	creepy	感じ悪い
high	高い	strange	変
spacious	広い	mysterious	神秘的

Q. Do you think _____ places are scary?

A. Yes, I do. / No, I think _____ places are scary? / I am never scared.

Toolbox 3

When were you scared?

いつこわいでしたか？

alone in the dark	くらい場所で一人	going to the dentist	歯医者に行く
watching horror movies	ホラー映画を見ている	meeting a famous person	芸能人と出会う
walking home	家に帰る	staying home alone	一人で家に
going to the doctor	医者に行く	flying on a plane	飛行機を乗る

Q. When were you scared?

A. When I was _____.

Fears / phobias

How many do you know?

A
Aichmophobia - Fear of needles or pointed objects..
Atychiphobia - Fear of failure.
Autophobia - Fear of being alone.

B
Bacteriophobia - Fear of bacteria.
Belonephobia - Fear of pins and needles.

C
Catoptrophobia - Fear of mirrors.
Claustrophobia - Fear of confined spaces.
Coulrophobia - Fear of clowns.

D
Dentophobia - Fear of dentists.

E
Entomophobia - Fear of insects.
Ephebiphobia - Fear of teenagers.

G
Gamophobia - Fear of marriage.
Glossophobia - Fear of speaking in public.

H
Hemophobia - Fear of blood.
Hydrophobia - Fear of water.

I
Iatrophobia - Fear of doctors.
Insectophobia - Fear of insects.

K
Koinoniphobia - Fear of rooms.

L
Lilapsophobia - Fear of tornadoes and hurricanes.
Lockiophobia - Fear of childbirth.

M
Mageirocophobia - Fear of cooking.
Megalophobia - Fear of large things.
Microphobia - Fear of small things.
Mysophobia - Fear of dirt and germs.

N
Necrophobia - Fear of death or dead things.
Noctiphobia - Fear of the night.
Nosocomephobia - Fear of hospitals.
Nyctophobia - Fear of the dark.

O
Obesophobia - Fear of gaining weight.
Ophidiophobia - Fear of snakes.

P
Pathophobia - Fear of disease.
Pedophobia - Fear of children.
Pteromerhanophobia - Fear of flying.
Pyrophobia - Fear of fire.

S
Scolionophobia - Fear of school.
Selenophobia - Fear of the moon.
Sociophobia - Fear of social evaluation.
Somniphobia - Fear of sleep.

T
Tachophobia - Fear of speed.
Technophobia - Fear of technology.
Tonitrophobia - Fear of thunder.
Trypanophobia - Fear of needles / injections.

V-Z
Venustraphobia - Fear of beautiful women.
Verminophobia - Fear of germs.
Wiccaphobia - Fear of witches and witchcraft.
Xenophobia - Fear of strangers or foreigners.
Zoophobia - Fear of animals.

My Nightmare 私の悪夢

Dialog – "The creepy old house"

> There was a creepy old house in my neighborhood when I was growing up.

> Really? What was it like? Did you go inside?

> I was often going inside. It was a deserted old house. Sometimes my friends were with me. We were playing inside the house together at night. It was dark and creepy.

> There was an old school in my neighborhood when I was growing up. Many people were hearing strange noises at night coming from there.

意味

現在進行形は＜be 動詞＋〜ing＞の形でしたが、過去進行形では＜be 動詞過去＋〜ing＞の形になります。意味は「（そのとき）〜していした」です。現在進行形を過去形にするだけなので、現在進行形を理解してからのステップが望ましいです。

例文：[現在進行形]

He is playing baseball.（彼はテニスをしています。）

[過去進行形]

He was playing baseball.（彼はテニスをしていました。）

2 now を then に

現在進行形で使われていた now（今）は、過去進行形になると then（そのとき）にします。 また then のかわりに、「at that time」としても同じ意味です。

例文：[現在進行形]

I am doing my homework now.（私は今宿題をしています。）

[過去進行形]

I was doing my homework then.（私はそのとき宿題をしていました。）

Stage 13 — One with English コミュニケーションコース
My Nightmare 私の悪夢

Interview and Introductions
面接と紹介
"My Nightmare"

面接 自分で文章で答えましょう。	
質問	答え
1. What do you fear?	
2. What kinds of places are scary?	
3. When were you scared?	

相手の答えを書きましょう。	
質問	答え
4. What do you fear?	
5. What kinds of places are scary?	
6. When were you scared?	

友達の趣味を紹介しましょう。

This is my friend _____（名前）.

He/She fears _____.

He/She thinks _____ places are scary.

He/She was scared when he/she was _____.

My Nightmare 私の悪夢

まず be 動詞を○して
下線に（）の中の動詞を ING 形書きましょう。

1. What (were / was) they _____ for dinner? (have)
2. I (were / was) _____ a book. (read)
3. The children (was / were) _____ dodge ball. (play)
4. The dog (was / were) _____ under the table. (sit)
5. (Was / Were) Tim and Allen _____ again? (argue)

Was/were + ~ing 形を使って疑問文を書きましょう。必要であれば **what/why/where/when** も使いましょう。

（例：Q: **(you / live)**　　Where were you living in 1990?

　　　 A: **In South Africa.**

1. Q: (you / do) _____ at 11 o'clock?
   A: I was sleeping.
2. (it / rain) _____ when you got up?
   A: No, it was sunny.
3. (Eric / walk) _____ so fast?
   A: He was late for class.
4. (Cindy / wear) _____ a suit yesterday?
   A: No, it was a dress.

Stage 13 One with English コミュニケーションコース

My Nightmare 私の悪夢

Read, read, read

Read the following and answer the questions.
下の書いてあることを読んで質問を答えましょう。

I sometimes had scary dreams when I was growing up. I was often dreaming about scary things and having nightmares when I was sick. I had many scary dreams when I had a fever. Once I had a really scary dream. I was walking on a dark and quiet road. There was a car on the road far away. It was coming very fast. There was a scary sound coming from the car. I was trying to run away from the car, but I couldn't run very fast. I was falling down again and again. The car was getting close and the sound was getting very loud. I was trying to wake up. Just before the car hit me, I woke up. When I woke up, I was breathing heaving and sweating. I was happy it was just a nightmare.		
1. When does Eric have nightmares?	2. What was Eric doing when the car is coming?	3. Do you think this nightmare is scary? Why?

Write, write, write

Write about a nightmare or scary dream.
あなたの悪夢について書きましょう。何の場所？何をしていましたか？

www.ingramcontent.com/pod-product-compliance
Lightning Source LLC
Chambersburg PA
CBHW041544220426
43665CB00002B/30